William Ralph Inge

Society in Rome Under the Caesars

Vol. 1

William Ralph Inge

Society in Rome Under the Caesars
Vol. 1

ISBN/EAN: 9783337379391

Printed in Europe, USA, Canada, Australia, Japan

Cover: Foto ©ninafisch / pixelio.de

More available books at **www.hansebooks.com**

SOCIETY IN ROME

UNDER

THE CÆSARS.

By WILLIAM RALPH INGE, M.A.,

FELLOW OF KING'S COLLEGE, CAMBRIDGE, AND
ASSISTANT MASTER AT ETON.

NEW YORK:

CHARLES SCRIBNER'S SONS,

1888.

PREFACE.

———◆———

THIS Essay obtained the "Hare Prize" at Cambridge in 1886, the subject chosen by the Examiners being "The Social Life of Rome in the 1st Century, A.D." It is now published with a few alterations and corrections, but nearly in its original form.

W. R. I.

Jan. 1888.

TABLE OF CONTENTS.

INTRODUCTORY.

CHAPTER I.

RELIGION.

CHAPTER II.

PHILOSOPHY.

CHAPTER III.

MORALITY.

CHAPTER IV.

THE GOVERNMENT AND SOCIETY.

CHAPTER V.

LITERATURE AND ART.

CHAPTER VI.

GRADES OF SOCIETY.

CHAPTER VII.

EDUCATION, MARRIAGE, &c.

a

CHAPTER X.

L U X U R Y.

INTRODUCTORY.

THE manners and customs of the Romans at the time of their greatest power and civilisation have naturally been made the subject of much research and many speculative treatises. They have been reconstructed in the minutest details from the evidence of those ancient authorities which time has spared us, and from the relics which excavation has continually been bringing to light. Thanks to the labours of scholars and archæologists in Germany and elsewhere, we can picture to ourselves many scenes of Roman life with as much clearness and accuracy as those which we see around us. The dress which the Roman citizen wore, the structure and furniture of the house in which he lived, the library in which he studied, the banquets in which he shared, have all

b

been described with a minuteness which leaves but little to be added. With equal accuracy and exhaustiveness, the names and functions of the different slaves, the ceremonies attending marriages and funerals, the position of the various buildings of public resort at Rome, have been discussed and determined, till there seems to be but little left for ingenuity to effect in the work of reconstruction, except by compelling the earth to yield up more of the treasures which she still hides beneath her surface.

To collect or endeavour to add to these details is not the purpose of this treatise. Such an attempt, if not utterly vain, would necessarily destroy the proportion of the parts, and encumber the pages with a mass of citation. Details of this kind can only be introduced in an essay of modest dimensions, where they seem required for the purpose of illustrating some larger feature of the subject. For the most part generalizations must take the place of minute description, and the subjective side of civilisation in the first century occupy more attention than the objective. If the really characteristic points in that civilisation can be seized, and the most important phenomena given their due prominence, the object of the essay will have been attained.

The scheme of arrangement which we have chosen will be easily understood from the headings of the chapters. Religion, Philosophy, and Morality, treated, as far as possible, in their social aspects, occupy the first place. Then follows a short chapter on the social influence of Imperialism in the first century. The Literature and Art of the the period are next considered, after which we have endeavoured to analyse Roman society into its component parts, discussing briefly the various grades into which the community was divided. Then descending more into detail, we have described the life of the individual, first tracing, in outline, the ordinary course of a Roman's career from the cradle to the grave, and then giving some account of the daily habits of the best-known sections of society. Public amusements form the subject of the next chapter, and the last contains a consideration of the luxury of the wealthy classes.

We subjoin a list of the chief modern works which we have consulted.

Becker. Gallus.

Capes. Early Empire. Stoicism.

Champagny. Les Césars.

Coulanges. La Cité Antique.

Dureau de la Malle. L'Economie Politique des Romains.

Freeman. Essays, vol. 2.

Furneaux. Tacitus' Annals, Introd.

Friedländer. Sittengeschichte Roms.

Froude. Short Studies, 3.

Gibbon. Decline and Fall.

Guhl and Koner. Life of Greeks and Romans.

Lecky. History of European Morals.

Marquardt. Das Privatleben der Römer.

Merivale. History.

Seeley. Essays.

Wallon. L'Esclavage dans l'Antiquité.

CHAPTER I.

R E L I G I O N.

THE national religion of the Roman people was a part of the polity of the republic. The gods were among the possessions of the burgess body, and their protection was one of the privileges which citizenship conferred. As was natural, the abode of the divinities bore a close resemblance to the earthly city under their care. Every natural phenomenon, every mental conception, had its counterpart in the world of gods. These gods were not, like those of the Greeks, transformed into living personalities, with definite characters and varied histories. They were vaguely conceived abstractions, which never acquired palpable substance. Equally removed from anthropomorphism and from mysticism, the Roman religion never developed either a mythology or a secret cult, nor did the intellectual or philosophic spirit exercise itself greatly in the manufacture of reli-

A

gious symbolism. The gods remained dimly conceived personifications of their eponymous qualities, realities indeed to the many, but not possessed
of any attributes to captivate the imagination or
to kindle moral enthusiasm. Neither imagination
nor enthusiasm were congenial to the Roman
spirit, and that spirit was faithfully reproduced in
the national belief. The relations between man
and God were conceived in a thoroughly practical
and utilitarian, not to say commercial spirit. The
legal formulism, which it is the pride of Rome to
have developed, invaded from the earliest date the
province of religion. The moral law as promul-
gated under the sanction of religion resembled a
code rather than deductions from a principle. The
service of the gods generally consisted in a kind of
bargaining, in which the worshipper expected to
receive full value, generally in kind, for every act
of homage and devotion. It was possible occasionally to overreach a benignant deity, and on the
other hand it was necessary for the worshipper to
avoid any mistakes in form which might enable
the god to evade his part of the contract. This
explains the function of the pontiffs, who acted as
professors of spiritual jurisprudence ; not as media-

tors between the contracting parties, but as advisers retained by the human suppliant. Unworthy as this conception of religion is, it was not without real usefulness to the Roman community.' The gods were not less truly believed in because their natures were dimly conceived, and their attributes of a not very exalted character. The offender against the moral law was felt to be severely punished by the simple anathema which declared him *sacer*, and no longer under the protection of the Capitoline Jupiter. Though in itself a cold and uninspiring faith, it derived strength and warmth from its connection with the civic body. It was no galling chain, but a veritable alliance that bound the Roman church to the Roman state. Religion found its noblest expression in patriotism, and patriotism its sanction and support in religion.

The doctrine of a future life, so important as a moral influence in all societies, shared at Rome the vagueness which characterised the other religious beliefs of the people. No legends of heroes and demigods bridged over the chasm between mortality and the world of spirits.* The existence

* Such stories as afterwards appeared bear evident traces of their foreign origin.

of the soul after death was held rather as a theory than as a dogma* ; and we seldom find it used in an argument without a parenthetical apology such as "if the common belief be true." Such a half-hearted faith could have little effect on life or conduct. We should remember, however, that the educated persons, whose writings have come down to us, are not fair representatives of the mass of the people. The righteous indignation with which Lucretius attacks the fables about hell, current among the vulgar, seems to show that belief in a future punishment was strong enough to cause considerable trouble and unhappiness in the minds of many. It is indeed curious that, so far as belief in immortality existed at Rome, it acted not as an almost necessary consolation, as in modern Christian societies, but as a gloomy and tormenting apprehension, the desire for continued existence being neutralised by the fear of Minos and Cerberus. In other words, while our tendency is to dwell exclusively on the brighter side of the doctrine, the ancients seem seldom to have sought

* The remark of Champagny, "Pour lui " (the Roman) "l'immortalité de la famille et de la patrie remplaçait l'immortalité de son âme," shews a profound comprehension of the spirit of Paganism.

pleasure or consolation in the anticipation of future happiness, and to have vexed their souls by gloomy forebodings of the infernal regions.

The Roman religion was not radically altered by the various foreign elements that became incorporated with it. The gloomy faith of the Etruscans, the genial mythology of the Greeks, the fanatical mysticism of Asia, all left their mark on the liberal religion of the conquering republic, always ready to tolerate and find room for the various gods of the nations whom the sword of the legions had ejected from their homes. But so long as the Capitol remained the centre of Roman religion, and Romans were Romans by blood and not by adoption, the foundations of the national religion continued firm, and withstood the assaults of foreign divinities. Greek and oriental gods were allowed their places in heaven, as their votaries were permitted to reside at Rome, but conquest had discredited both alike, and gods as well as men were expected to acknowledge their superiors. In the case of Greece, indeed, the process of identifying the two celestial companies won acceptance, the identification being in some cases true, in others fictitious. But Jupiter Capitolinus refused to array himself in the garb of Olympian Zeus, nor did Venus Cloacina readily adapt herself to the character of Idalian Aphrodite. Still less could the Phrygian mother of the gods, with her mutilated priests and ecstatic orgies, find a place in the sober and dignified assemblage of Latin deities. Her worship, when at length it took root in Rome, found its congenial soil among the "stepsons of Italy," who were silently swamping the good old stock, and it was as a heresy or new religion that it appeared, not as a part of the national faith. Pliant and liberal as that faith appeared, it was in reality conservative, unchanging, and incapable of development. It flourished while its creators maintained their vigour and their national unity: it decayed when corruption and division had weakened that vigour and dissolved that unity: it flickered now and again with a semblance of vitality as Rome made fitful efforts to return to her former self; and it finally expired with the last throes of the sovereign nation, maintaining to the last that exclusive civic character which had been its strength and was now its weakness.

The type of character which this religion tended

to produce was ·rather dignified than attractive, rather admirable than amiable. The unselfish impulses, the self-sacrifice, which are the food of all religion, took the form of national *esprit de corps,* and worked exclusively within that narrow limit. Humanity in the larger sense found hardly any place in the moral code. The sphere of duty was the state, and its miniature the family. Courage, self-devotion, industry, frugality, were practised or admired as civic virtues, conducive to the welfare of the community. Piety towards the gods and obedience to the magistrates were duties of the same kind. Marriage and education were public duties, to be performed in no self-regarding spirit. The result was a somewhat hard, but very strong national character. Duty was ever present, and asserted itself in every act of life. No doubt or conflict of motives was possible. Divided allegiance could not be thought of while Jove and the city of Rome remained* to claim the service of the citizen : in life or in death the Roman belonged not to himself, but to the state. It was this that carried the Roman power over three continents,

---

* Incolumi Jove et urbe Roma, *Hor.* The expression is highly characteristic.

and enabled the city on the Tiber to attain its unique position. Never since the fall of Paganism have the civic virtues shone out so brilliantly : never since, perhaps, have religion and patriotism made so potent an alliance.

The foregoing remarks will have indicated to some extent the causes of the decline of religion which marked the last century of the republic and the succeeding period. Moral enthusiasm was never excited by the national religion except in the form of patriotism, and the expansion of the empire had made patriotism a less absorbing principle than heretofore. Self-sacrifice seemed hardly necessary, when Rome was already mistress of the world. The privileges of citizenship were now so apparent and so great that its obligations naturally fell into the background. The Roman no longer felt himself a member of a militant community ; he was the possessor of a rich inheritance, which his ancestors had won for him to enjoy. Thus the living spark which had kept alive the smouldering fire of Roman faith was nearly extinguished. It was certain that the unattractive dogmas which remained would not command much respect after it was gone. Nor was the prosperity of the Empire the only reason for the decay of patriotic faith. The constant influx of foreigners from every quarter of the world, especially from the East, was fatal to the national religion. Neither natural propensities nor tradition led these new-comers to embrace the religion of their conquerors. None but Romans could be faithful worshippers of the Roman gods. The old stock, an ever-decreasing minority, could make no stand against an invasion of aliens often intellectually their superiors, who brought with them not merely cosmopolitan indifference, but the powerful destructive force of Greek philosophy. Among the educated classes the combined influence of these two causes made rapid havoc of the old faith. The tendency to materialism was increased by the corrupt and licentious life that had become common through wealth and idleness. The moral sense, always restricted within narrow limits, was blunted by the institution of slavery and the other injustices of irresponsible power. In most cases the simple faith of former days was as completely obsolete as the frugal fare of the citizen-farmer. The belief in immortality was openly ridiculed. In Cicero's time hardly an old woman could be found, if we

believe the writer, who trembled at the fables
about the infernal regions.* Even boys, says
Juvenal, disbelieve in the world of spirits.† The
existence of the gods, according to these and
other writers, was commonly treated as an open
question, and one of not very great importance.
The rites of religion were either neglected or performed in a perfunctory and contemptuous manner.
The majority either denied moral obligation, or
attached it to some system of philosophy. The
old religion as a moral force seemed quite spent
and gone.

We must however be careful not to accept the
statements of our authorities too strictly. The
leading writers of any age are seldom the truest
exponents of the beliefs of the masses. The
attacks of freethought and philosophy do not
readily reach the uneducated. Such expressions
as those of Cicero and Juvenal above referred to,
are often hastily made, and must be weighed with
due caution. There are many indications that
upon the lower classes at least religion still had a
considerable hold. It is, perhaps, unsafe to lay
too much stress on the very numerous monuments

* Cic. de N. D. 2. 2.   † Juvenal, S. 2. 149.

that have been found expressing a belief in a future life, for experience tells us that pious or kindly insincerity haunts the tomb unblamed ; but it is fair to mention these as a set off against the inscriptions of ostentatious materialism and the vaunts of shallow philosophy. A more convincing proof of the abiding vitality of the old Polytheism is furnished by the power which it still possessed of assimilating new elements, drawn from the religions of the East and of barbarian countries. Even newly-created divinities from time to time appeared, but these were usually deceased or living emperors, who owed their elevation rather to flattery than to faith. The obstinate resistance which Paganism offered to Christianity has also been justly quoted as indicating a firmer hold on the old religion than we generally attribute to its later votaries. The struggle between the two religions cannot be said to have begun in earnest till after the close of our period ; but we cannot form a fair estimate of the state of opinion in the first century without drawing upon later as well as earlier history. The tenacity of the old beliefs when brought into contact with Christianity is often remarkable, and still more so is the attitude

of the earlier Christians to Paganism. Jupiter, and
Venus, and Apollo were commonly regarded not
as fictions but as really existing evil spirits, by no
means absolutely powerless. Even Pagan divination was believed to be a genuine intercourse with
the spiritual world. Hence, to do homage to an
idol was an actual treason to the Supreme Being.
These indications shew that positive faith was by
no means a thing of the past among the Pagans of
the empire. The subject which we shall now enter
upon ought to give us a more definite idea of the
state of religion in our period.

The belief that the will of the gods was in many
different ways communicated to mankind formed
a very important part of the religion both of
Greece and Rome. In Greece the oracles, at
Rome the augurs and haruspices, in both the
astrologers and interpreters of dreams, were
believed to have the power of explaining the
intentions and wishes of heaven to men. Portents and prodigies were vouchsafed, it was
believed, as warnings in times of danger. Appari-
tions of the gods in human form were authenticated
in various places and times. Miracles of healing
and exhibitions of supernatural power were not

unknown. In short, to the pious or superstitious Pagan, the gods were constantly making their presence felt in the daily order of things, and it became the believer to be always watchful for the heaven-sent signs which might have been intended by a gracious providence to save him from ruin or lead him to fortune.

The attitude which the educated world adopted towards these widespread superstitions is very remarkable. On the one hand the historians duly chronicle every prodigy or monstrous birth that they find related in their authorities, so that these absurdities fill a space in their works which it would be difficult to parallel in any other secular histories. On the other, there is no lack of the most contemptuous disbelief in the whole system, expressed in no doubtful terms, by the contemporaries of the historians who apparently attach so much importance to it. On the one hand we find Celsus, in the era of the Antonines, basing his chief argument against Christianity on the numerous and well-attested miracles of Paganism, and especially on the innumerable instances of fulfilled prophecies; while on the other Cicero in his work on Divination appeals with equal con-

fidence to the facts of history on the other side,
recalling how Cæsar crossed over into Africa in
opposition to the auspices, and by so doing prevented his enemies from uniting against him,
while his unsuccessful antagonist never failed to
obey the warnings of the haruspices; and how
throughout the civil war these predictions either
remained unfulfilled, or were directly falsified.*
We find the same writer, himself an augur, quoting
with approval Cato's saying that he wondered how
one augur could meet another without laughing,
and Pliny the Younger sarcastically suggested that
apparently many dreams are meant to be inter-
preted by contraries.† Innumerable instances of
the most absurd and childish superstitions are
recorded even of men of strong sense and practical
ability, while at the same time we might quote
passages condemning these superstitions in an
enlightened manner.

With regard to the historians, some allowance
must be made for the idea of history then prevailing. The ancient writers of history endeavoured to be at once dramatic and didactic. The
narrative of the past was often made a peg on

* Cic. de Div. 2. 24.　　　　　† Plin. Ep. 1. 18.

which to hang the author's rhetorical displays and his views of morality and the economy of the world. Both these purposes were in a measure served by the introduction of the supernatural, which can be easily made picturesque, and, to the believer, instructive. Prodigies were equally useful to point a moral and to adorn a tale. Livy admits that the number of these miracles varies exactly with the credulity of the people among whom they occur ;* but he excuses himself in another place by saying that when he is narrating ancient events his mind "takes somehow an ancient cast,"† which makes such stories seem appropriate and pleasing, and that it does not seem to him right to pass over with contempt events which the good men of former days believed and preserved. And if Livy, a writer of a poetical and uncritical temperament, feels it necessary to apologise for transcribing the records of portents, we are not surprised to find that in Tacitus the mentions of them are few and far between. For such as do occur custom may perhaps be partly responsible; and we in our own day must have often noticed the peculiar half-respectful, half-contemptuous defer-

---

* Liv. 24. 10.   † Liv. 43. 13.

ence which philosophers and freethinkers in general show to popular superstitions, a deference which approaches what used to be called chivalry. Modern histories furnish many parallels to Tacitus in this respect.

It would however be a great mistake to suppose that disbelief in the supernatural was the rule among the educated classes. In some form or other the natural tendency of the human mind to such beliefs generally asserted itself. Religion had never been a great moral force in itself at Rome, and now its alliance with patriotism was being dissolved : nothing remained but lifeless ritual and the myriad forms of superstition, which only usurp the name of religion. It was however in the form of superstition that Paganism now chiefly lived on. It is here, and here only, that we find the fear of the gods influencing human action. The man of pleasure, who scoffed at the idea of moral retribution for the grossest of his crimes, trembled at a serpent in his path, and paid an Oriental astrologer to read his fortune. An eclipse still caused a panic in the Imperial legions. The despot, who trampled without scruple on every law, human or divine, was accustomed to crawl under his bed at the sound of thunder.* To "enquire into the years" of the emperor's life was high treason. Every form of spiritualism had its hierophants. Rome swarmed with quacks and impostors from every corner of the empire, who made a handsome profit out of the credulity of their masters. The women were even more addicted to these absurditi.s than the men, and Roman ladies were often the slaves of an astute priest or astrologer. Scarcely anyone was strong-minded enough to reject the whole mass of superstition. Even Pliny the Elder considered that there might be something in dreams, and the majority never thought of questioning their truth as predictions of the future. Incapable for the most part of influencing any action for good, this melancholy substitute for religion continued to vex the souls of men and women, and divert their thoughts from any impulse towards a higher life. It was the fate of Paganism thus to drift into dreary shallows when cut adrift from the anchor which had bound it to the citadel of Romulus.

The anxious search for spiritual food sometimes led men to wander beyond the precincts of the

* Suet. Cal. 2.

Roman Olympus. Isis and Serapis already numbered many votaries of both sexes in the first century. It was a common complaint that the gods of despised Eastern nations were usurping the honours of Capitoline Jove. Legislative enactments were called into play in the vain hope of stopping the advancing tide. Throughout the period alien worships came more and more into vogue, and were embraced with an enthusiasm which contrasted painfully with the languid conformity of the orthodox. The causes of this movement lay far too deep to be touched by the legislator. For the last hundred and fifty years (I speak of the middle of our period) the dry ethics of Stoicism and the negations of Epicureanism had practically divided the Roman mind between them. We need not go into the causes, already partly discussed, which made a reaction in favour of positive and emotional religion natural and inevitable. It will be enough to mention the influence of Alexandria, the influx of Orientals into Rome, the decrease of the Roman stock, and the inherent inability of the systems above mentioned to meet the requirements of the human mind. These requirements seemed to be satisfied by the mystic religions of the East, which subordinated the intellect to the emotions, and were based not on reasoning but on ecstacy: which regarded the body as a disgrace or burden, and pleasure as an evil; which substituted a new ideal for the civic virtues that had lost their cogency, and again held out the bright hope of a future life, which had been growing dimmer and fainter through the long period of hardness and indulgence. Like all other moral and social revolutions, this change began from the lower strata of society. The slaves, the poor, the unprivileged, the expatriated, were the first to turn for consolation to the new source opened to them. Among them the monotheistic creeds of the East first took root; among them Judaism made its proselytes, and Christianity its earliest converts. But the movement was not long in extending itself to the rich and powerful. Already in our period we have indications which in the light of succeeding history we can read, as shewing the growing influence of Alexandria and Palestine. The gentleness which tempers the stoicism of Seneca, the almost feminine sweetness of Epictetus, the affection and resignation of Quintilian under domestic bereavement, the complaints in Juvenal of the spread of Jewish and

Oriental superstitions, the edicts banishing Jews from Rome, are signs of various kinds which might escape our notice if we had not later events to help us. With those events we need not hesitate to ascribe them to that influence which, even then at work and powerful, though obscure and little noticed, was at last to overthrow the temples of the Pagan gods, and establish Christianity as the religion of the Empire.

To sum up briefly the results arrived at in this chapter, the national religion of Rome derived its force as a moral principle from its alliance with the civic spirit. That spirit from various causes had declined, and religion in consequence became a routine of barren ritual, or a vehicle of puerile superstition. Among the educated the prevailing tone was a careless Agnosticism, which tolerated religion as a serviceable instrument for guiding the vulgar mind, but was itself by no means exempt from the popular superstitions. The uneducated masses still retained their faith in the gods, but the influence of their religion on their morality was almost nil. A crowd of superstitions kept the spiritual world constantly in their minds, but in a manner that could exercise no wholesome influence

on their character. In this unhappy condition men
began to turn to the East, and to fall under the influence of the mystical and ecstatic worships which
were there indigenous. The moral revolution thus
begun ramified first chiefly among the despised
classes, but before the close of the first century
had begun to attract educated minds whom the
Græco-Roman philosophies of the Stoa and of
Epicurus could no longer satisfy.

CHAPTER II.

PHILOSOPHY.

ONE of the consequences of the defective and unsatisfying character of Roman religion was the importance and prominence of moral philosophy. Men turned to Stoicism or Epicureanism to supply them with a rule of life which they could not find in the worship of the gods. So completely was that worship dissociated from ethical teaching, that it was left for philosophers to evolve and inculcate that important function of religion. The social influence of moral philosophy was therefore infinitely greater than at the present day, when the majority find in religion all the guidance that they need.

Two systems of philosophy, Stoicism and Epicureanism, flourished at Rome in the first century. To these perhaps we should add the Neo-Pythagorean School, which ultimately gave birth to the New Platonism of Alexandria. It may, however,

be said that philosophy at Rome in the first
century means Stoicism, so completely did the
doctrines of Zeno—transplanted, not without modification, into Roman soil—overshadow all other
systems of ethics. Stoicism was in fact very well
suited to the Roman temperament. Abandoning
the transcendental part of Greek Stoicism, the
Romans found in the austere renunciations and
rigid dogmatism of the system a rule well suited
to the hardness of their national temperament.
The ideal Roman character, which still lived in
theory, and was occasionally even now almost
realised in a Thrasea or an Arria, was very much
like that of the stoic "sage." Inflexible devotion
to virtue, imperturbable serenity of temperament,
contempt of worldly goods and misfortunes, justice
to others without sympathy, were Roman qualities
and stoic maxims : and even the stoic conception
of the Deity—half monotheistic, half pantheistic,
though it did not enter much into the Neo-Stoicism
of Rome—was hardly alien to the spirit of Roman
religion. But the constraining power which Stoicism
exerted lay in its assertion of abstract right and
duty, the duty of "living according to nature," as
they expressed it, that is, of fulfilling the law of

our being, which is to follow virtue and virtue
alone, "in scorn of consequence," and to rise superior to all the changes and chances of mortal life,
which are not really evils, for "there is nothing bad,
but thinking makes it so," except vice. It would
be easy to illustrate the sublimity of this doctrine
from the writings and actions of its votaries ; easy
also to shew how attractive it must have been to
men living under a corrupt despotism, where a good
man had to be "a law unto himself," and independent of his surroundings for noble life and
mental happiness. Stoicism was in fact a noble
witness against some of the worst tendencies of
the age. It was, in the first place, a standing protest against materialism. In a period when everyone hunted wealth and comfort with a feverish
activity, it declared that the sage alone is rich,
happy, and powerful : that the millionaire on his
banquet-couch may be in far worse case than the
slave on the rack,* and that everything which the
world deems valuable is ἀδιάφορον, indifferent, unworthy of the attention of a wise man. Again, it
necessarily tended to break down the barriers of

* "Jacere in convivio malum est, torqueri in eculeo bonum, si
illud turpiter hoc honeste fit." Sen. Ep. 71.

classes. The consistent Stoic must admit that his slaves may be his superiors, and cannot treat them as mere chattels. In its logical conclusion, Stoicism meant the natural equality of all mankind. Seneca is often led into expressions which imply this, and Epictetus in the true Christian tone says, "We are all brothers, because we are God's children." The growth of humanity in the latter half of the century, which will occupy us in part of the next chapter, and especially the increasing gentleness to slaves, was in no small degree the work of stoic philosophy. Lastly, Stoicism operated in placing before men a purer conception of God. Let us quote, first, Persius' energetic protest against the *commercial* view of sacrifice which we mentioned in the last chapter,

> " Compositum jus fasque animo, sanctosque recessus
> Mentis, et incoctum generoso pectus honesto.
> Hanc cedo ut admoveam templis, et farre litabo."*

and then refer to—we have not space to quote— the numerous and beautiful maxims of Seneca, which made Christian apologists claim him as "sæpe noster." Shadowy and scarcely personal as the stoic deity was, his attributes were far

* Pers. 2. ad fin.

more divine than those of the objects of popular
worship.

Great as were the merits of Stoicism, its defects
were equally great, and inseparable from its
character. The minds of the Romans at this time
were only too receptive of these faults. What can
be more startling than the arrogance of philosophy
towards heaven ? It was the boast of the sage
" to fear neither man nor God":* " from man,"
says Seneca in another place, " not much is to be
feared, from God nothing ":† " the wise man sur-
veys mankind from above, the gods from an equal
level":‡ nay, in some respects the sage even
excels the Deity, for "his wisdom is his own
making, while God is wise by nature."§ Nor was
it all humanity, as we see, that was thus exalted to
an equality with the gods. In spite of the level-
ling doctrines which philosophers sometimes enun-
ciated, their system was really rigidly exclusive.
The masses, who were ignorant of philosophy,
were classed as slaves and madmen, nor did their
abject condition move the pity of the sage, but
rather ministered to his spiritual pride. Pride, in

* Ep. 75.   † Sen. Ben. 7. 1.
‡ Ep. 41.   § Ep. 53.

fact, was the foundation of much of the stoical system, and formed one of its chief attractions. Almost more serious was the destruction of the sympathies and affections, never too warm at Rome, which formed a definite part of stoic teaching. " To feel pain at the misfortunes of others," says Seneca, " is a weakness unworthy of the wise man. . . . Only weak eyes become inflamed at the sight of ophthalmia in other men."*
Feeling was in fact altogether despised, while intellect was enthroned in the seat of divinity. *Knowledge* of good and evil was the aim and object of life. " Una re consummatur animus, scientia bonorum et malorum." " In Deo nihil extra animum ; totus ratio est."† The result was a hardness and narrowness of character which prevented it from ever reaching perfection. The practical moralist might also complain that the porch offered no sufficient *motive* for a virtuous life. In the sublimity of its ideal it forgot the facts of human nature. It reproved vices, but could not correct them. It seemed to be made up of inconsistencies throughout. It exhorted men to live according to nature, while it repressed the

* Sen. Clem. 2. 6.   † Sen. Nat. Queest.

affections and renounced the pleasures which
nature bids us follow.   It professed a pious humi-
lity, while it exalted its votaries to a level with
the Deity.   It declared that all men were brothers,
and at the same time classed all but its own sect as
slaves, fools, and madmen.   It preached resignation to the will of heaven, and at the same time
counselled men to terminate their existence whenever life ceased to satisfy them.*   It was in fact
a narrow, one-sided, and withal a hopeless creed,
which might give a rule of life to the noble-minded,
but could do little to regenerate society.

We have quoted Seneca so often in this chapter
that we must say a few words about his position
as a Stoic.   It has been said with truth that
Stoicism was no part of Seneca's nature.   He accepted it with his intellect, but his heart led him
constantly to contradict its principles.   Hence the
inconsistencies with which he has been twitted.
His tastes, character, and affections often revolted
against the doctrines of his school.   When he says,

* Stoicism is largely responsible for the epidemics of suicide
which characterised this period, cf. Sen. Ep. 71. "Sæpe et fortiter
pereundum est, *neque maximis de causis,* nam nec maximæ sunt
quæ nos terrent."   Suicide was, in fact, almost the logical consequence of the stoical view of the state of the world.

" No good thing can be enjoyed without a friend to share it," it is the man, not the philosopher, who speaks. But we need not delay to reconcile the inconsistencies in Seneca's character. Perhaps Garat was right in saying that we should understand it if we lived under a reign of terror, such as that of Nero or Robespierre.

It is more our business to consider the causes of the undoubted unpopularity of Stoicism with the government and with society in general. As regards the former, it would be difficult to find any justification for the charges of disloyalty against which Seneca defends philosophy. It does not appear that as a class the Stoics ever encouraged rebellion or disaffection. And yet we find that until after Domitian, philosophers were constantly regarded with disfavour, and occasionally persecuted and driven from Rome. Probably the government had an instinctive feeling that the spirit of Stoicism was hostile to despotism. A moral ideal, capable of leading men to self-sacrifice and contempt of comfort, was naturally distrusted by a monarchy which rested on materialism. Imperialism might secure wealth and ease to its subjects, but it gave no scope for lofty aspirations. Accordingly it instinctively

arrayed itself against both Stoicism and Christianity.
As regards popular opinion, the reasons for the
feeling against philosophy lie more on the surface.
People do not like the presence of an arrogant and
severe class of censors, especially when in spite of
some exaggerations their strictures are mainly just.
The man of pleasure always hates ideas, and the
man of the world generally despises arts which do
not tend to tangible advantage.   Hence the peculiar acrimony with which rhetoricians attacked
philosophy.   Again, in the latter half of the century, shams and humbugs became very frequent.
Just as many a sturdy beggar in the Middle Ages
donned the cowl of the begging friar, many an idle
vagabond and profligate called himself a Stoic, and
brought discredit upon the name.*   And even in
higher circles there often seemed the greatest inconsistency between the professions and the practice of the philosopher.   It often seemed that
while the Stoic disdained to help his fellow men,
he had a keen eye for his own profit.   We may
be sure that the career of Seneca evoked from his
contemporaries the same sarcasms with which

---

* See Tac. Ann. 16. 32, for Egnatius, a hypocrite of this class,
and Grant, Ethics 1. 281 ; Lightfoot, Ep. to Philippians, p. 284.

Macaulay has treated it. " The business of a philosopher was to declaim in praise of poverty with
two millions sterling out at usury : to meditate
epigrammatic conceits about the evils of luxury in
gardens which moved the envy of sovereigns ; to
rant about liberty, while fawning on the insolent
and pampered freedmen of a tyrant ; to celebrate
the divine beauty of virtue with the same pen
which had just before written a defence of the
murder of a mother by a son." Lastly, the sordid
habits and ostentatious disregard of the amenities
of life which many philosophers affected, must
have caused disgust and aversion in ordinary
society. In the second century their position
seems to have improved, both as regards the
government and public opinion.

But though generally unpopular, the philosopher
was by no means an outcast from society. He
was generally to be found in a large mansion,
acting almost like a private chaplain, instructing
in ethics those who wished to learn, and attending
the death-beds of members of the family. We
are particularly told that Petronius died without a
word of philosophy being spoken by his bedside;
and in his romance Trimalchio directs that no philo-

sopher is to be allowed to approach him during his
last illness.   These exceptions shew that the services of philosophy were usually enlisted in times
of trouble.   In most cases, no doubt, it was only
in such times that the man of the world troubled
himself much about the ideals of the sage. Mommsen's statement that the chief result of philosophy
was that "two or three families lived on frugal
fare to please the Stoa," seems, however, to be too
strong.   When we remember the numerous lectures, public and private, which celebrated philosophers gave to crowded audiences, the often important position held by confidential philosophers
at court, and the devoted affection which students
felt towards their teachers, as Persius for Cornutus,
we must admit a wider influence than these words
imply, at least in the latter half of our period.
Stoicism, in fact, held up the torch of morality in
a very dark age, and imperfect as it was both in
theory and practice, it testified always to the truth
of a moral ideal, and never ceased to point to virtue
as the one object of life.   Such a creed, though
disregarded by the many, can never exist in vain.
Society feels its influence even while it scorns its
professors.

CHAPTER III.

MORALITY.

THE subject of Morality, when treated, as we shall treat it, exclusively from the point of view of the social historian, divides itself naturally into three sections, Integrity, Humanity, and Purity. These simple headings seem to cover nearly all the topics which belong to the subject. We propose to take them in order, endeavouring in each case to come to some conclusion as to the state of public opinion and practice at the period with which we are concerned. The first two sections will be treated with as much detail as shall seem necessary to arrive at the required result; the last with that brevity and reticence which the nature of the subject demands.

The Romans of the Republic prided themselves greatly on their honesty and truthfulness. They were fond of contrasting their own 'fides' with the mendacity of the Greeks and the perfidy of the Phœnicians. Their annals were adorned with

signal examples of uprightness and fidelity, which,
though to a great extent fictitious, yet shew what
kind of qualities was most held in honour at the
time. The incorruptible Fabricius, the high-
minded Regulus, the frugal Cincinnatus, are examples of what Rome considered the highest
virtues in a citizen. The high estimation in which
integrity was held may be accounted for by the
early development of commerce in regal Rome ;*
and the defects in the conception of it which we
notice by the still narrow sphere in which contract
worked. The claims of *pietas* were satisfied by
the observance of stipulated forms ; and we hear
of gross frauds being perpetrated without blame
when the letter of the obligation was not violated.
This defective conception of the duty of honesty
would not be worth mentioning here if it had been
a mere rudimentary stage in the development of
contract ; but it continued to shew itself in the
dealings of Rome with foreign nations throughout
her history, and to a less extent in those between
private citizens.   Integrity was respected, but, like
other virtues, less for its own sake than as a law to
be observed.

* See Goldwin Smith's Essay on this subject.

Before the end of the Republic even this narrow morality had nearly ceased to be observed. Passionate love of money had overcome all respect for right and justice. We are startled by the universal corruption, the perjuries, forgeries, and other crimes committed for the sake of profit. Nor is much improvement visible after the beginning of our period. Perhaps there were fewer opportunities for crimes on a large scale than under the republic; but Juvenal, Tacitus, Seneca, and other writers, give a very gloomy picture of the unscrupulousness of society in money matters. As usual, the higher classes were probably the worst, but we hear complaints of the frequent dishonesty of tradesmen, and occasionally of great corruption in the middle class. The difficulty of making money by honest means, and the extravagant mode of life practised at Rome, gave a great stimulus both to legacy-hunting and forgery throughout society. The former of these was carried to such an extent that it is necessary to say a little about it. " Captatio," or the pursuit of inheritances, became a regular art at Rome, with established rules and methods. Persons existed who made it the one business of their lives to court some wealthy bachelor; to humour his fancies, praise his poetry, run his errands, make him presents, pray for his health and safety, and wait anxiously for his death. It was almost the only profession in which competition was keen and constant, and it appears to have been brought to great perfection. No means were thought degrading that could gain the wished-for end. The height of ingenuity was, perhaps, reached when the captator made a will of his own in favour of the rich old " orbus," and casually allowed him to see it. " Captatoria legata " had to be forbidden by law. The exist-ence of this contemptible class of men testifies to some of the worst evils of Roman society. The idleness of the citizens, their extravagance and luxury, their insatiable greed of money, above all, their habit of vicious celibacy, all contributed to make the odious figure of the captator so pro-minent in society. Pliny[*] laments the dege-neracy of his age in becoming terms. " Since senators and judges (he says) came to be chosen by their income, and magistrates and generals came to regard money as their chief title to dis-tinction; since childlessness came to exercise the

* Plin. H. N. 14. 5.

greatest authority and power, and legacy-hunting to be the most lucrative profession, all the noble pursuits of life and liberal arts have fallen to the ground, and servitude alone is profitable. In various ways all men care for money, and for money alone : even distinguished men prefer to cultivate the faults of others rather than their own virtues." " The whole town," says Petronius, "is divided into those who throw the bait and those who take it. No one acknowledges children ; for the man who has heirs is never invited to any festive gathering, but is left to associate with the dregs of society. On the other hand, the childless man is covered with honours, and passes for a model of all the virtues. Rome is like a field outside a plague-stricken city, in which you can see nothing but carcases and crows which feed upon them." So great were the advantages of childlessness that Seneca consoles a mother who had just lost her only son by reminding her of the greater consideration she will now enjoy.* A man who married was regarded as hardly in his senses.— " Certe sanus eras ? Uxorem, Postume, ducis ?" The captator, however, was sometimes tired of

* See also Tac. A. 3. 25, prævalida orbitate.

waiting, and after his fond prayers for his patron's
recovery had been unfortunately granted, he would
sometimes call in a *venefica* to hasten his possession of the inheritance, or in another case to remove
the remaining heir. Or if, as very often happened,
the vulture was baulked of his prey, and the inheritance left to a rival or a more worthy recipient,
the rejected flatterer might still make himself rich
and happy by means of a small tablet and mois-
tened signet.* It is impossible to explain away
the frequent notices of these crimes, and the
evidence they afford of an unscrupulous and corrupt spirit in society. The only question is how
far it extended. We would fain believe that in
many circles honour and integrity were the rule,
and this belief is supported by some works of the
period, *e.g.*, the letters of Pliny, which reveal a
high-minded and refined tone at least in their
author. Again, we do not hear much of dishonest
contract-work, or fraudulent adulterations, the
banes of modern commerce; and credit seems to
have been fairly good. The social and political
differences which separated classes of course led to
recognised unfairness on the part of the superior;

* Juv. 1. 67.

and the provinces were still impoverished by un-
equal trade with Roman merchants. This, however, was in process of improvement owing to the
extension of the citizenship, and the worst injustices belong to the end of the republican period.
On the whole it appears that public opinion was
decidedly laxer on this point than with us, and that
a considerable section, especially in the upper
classes, threw self-respect and scruples to the
winds, and pursued wealth with a cynical disregard
of right and wrong, such as is not often exhibited
openly in modern times.

The subject of humanity opens questions of
deeper interest, and demands a fuller investigation.
It forms indeed one of the most important branches
of our subject. We shall find that the first century
made substantial contributions to the progress of
humanity, and that the evidences we can collect
of opinion and practice on this head are full of interest and significance as bearing on the character
of social life at Rome. Cruelty may arise from
three causes. It may be a morbid passion which
feeds on the sight of suffering. Men who are free
from this disease may act cruelly either from
callousness or from vindictiveness, of which the

former may be called the masculine, the latter the feminine type of cruelty. The cruelty of the Romans belonged to the first class. Vindictiveness was not one of their national faults. When they were cruel, they were so from defective sensibility, which failed to make them realise the feelings and rights of their victims. This arose partly from a natural bluntness of character, partly from their narrow conception of the sphere of duty. Neither religion nor sympathy aroused in them a sense of the claims of aliens and dependents. Conscience in this as in other matters seemed the slave of positive law. The life of a prisoner, the land of a conquered city, were forfeited according to imme- morial law, and the right was exercised without scruple. A slave was a chattel, and his life was therefore of no value after he had ceased to be of use to his master. A debtor was made over by law to the power of his creditor, and mercy was seldom shewn to him. The whole history of Rome under the Republic is full of instances of what may be truly called *unfeeling* cruelty, of barbarities committed in cold blood and with- out remorse, as if the Twelve Tables were the highest code of justice and injustice, and the advantage of the Republic the ultimate test of right and wrong.

It is one of the most interesting features of the period we are now considering that it shews many evidences of awakening sensibility in this matter. It is not so much a real advance in morality, as an increase in the *sentiment* of humanity. We find public opinion going ahead of legislation, demanding the most lenient interpretation of the law, and sometimes insisting on legal right being waived in the interests of mercy. This tendency is especially noticeable in the case of slavery. In some other matters, such as the gladiatorial games, the awakening of the moral sense was longer deferred. For we trace only the first beginning of a change in public opinion, which required the sanction of a new religion to complete its development.

Let us pass in review the chief objects on which humanity may be practised, and see how the Romans of the first century dealt with them. To take first the case of slavery. There are several indications that in spite of the enormous increase in the number of slaves, their condition was better under the empire than under the Republic. We seldom hear of the seditions and revolts which endangered the state in the first and second centuries before Christ. The literature of the period gives several examples both of sincere and delicate friendship of the master towards the slaves, and of devotion and attachment of the slave to his master. Seneca insists strongly on the inherent equality of the master and his slaves, and entreats masters to consider "not how much the slave can be made to suffer with impunity, but how much the nature of right and justice permits. How much juster is it," he exclaims, "to treat men of noble mind and high character not as slaves, but as inferiors in social rank, to whom you stand in the position of protector not of owner. There are some things which the law permits, but which justice forbids to be done." Here we have an explicit recognition of extra-legal duty. Much of the credit of this improvement in feeling belongs to Stoicism, which preached the brotherhood of mankind with great persistency. It even succeeded in gaining for the slave-class several important legislative enactments, some of which fall within our period, others in the second century. Augustus, though he was himself guilty of the murder of a slave for killing a favourite quail, shewed his disapproval of atrocious cruelty by masters at least on one occasion. The anecdote, which supplies about the worst instance on record of Roman cruelty to slaves, is well-known. Vedius Pollio was about to throw a slave into his fish-pond to feed his lampreys, because he had broken a crystal cup. Augustus, as a punishment, ordered all the vessels in the house to be broken, and the pond to be filled up. The Lex Petronia, which forbade slaves to be exposed to fight with wild beasts without the sanction of a *judex*, is commonly placed in this reign. But the cause of mercy gained greater successes under the later Cæsars. Claudius forbade the exposition of sickly or infirm slaves on an island of the Tiber, and decreed, according to Suetonius, that those who killed their slaves instead of exposing them should be held guilty of murder (cædes), an ambiguous expression, for we cannot suppose that the offence was regarded in the same light as the murder of a free man. In fact, the power of life and death was not even limited till the reign of Antoninus. Nero appointed a judge to protect slaves from cruelty and outrage, a great step, if the law was honestly carried out. Domitian forbade the mutilation of slaves. The torture of slaves to extract evidence was about this time restricted, and seems to have become uncommon. The social position of the slave seems not quite so degraded as in the previous age. He appears more frequently in the educated professions, and is apparently allowed more liberty of action in the disposal of his time. It is common to allow him to purchase his freedom out of his savings, and if he is manumitted as a favour, he is generally allowed to retain his *peculium*. Manumission comes to be regarded as a regular reward of faithful service, and complaints are made of the dangerous extent to which it is practised. Altogether, Roman slavery at this time contrasts favourably in many ways with the negro slavery of some Christian nations. We do not forget the darker side of the picture. The atrocious execution of the 400 slaves of the murdered Pedanius in the reign of Nero,[*] the vengeance provoked by the harshness of Larcius Macedo at the end of the century,[†] the frequent murders of masters by their slaves,[‡] the frightful picture drawn by

---

[*] Tac. Ann. 14. 42–45.   [†] Plin. Ep. 3. 14.

[‡] Sen. Ep. 4. 8. "Non pauciores servorum ira cecidisse, quam regum."

Juvenal in his Sixth Satire, shew that a fearful power still remained in the master's hands, and that not a few abused it to a terrible extent. These horrors were, however, we believe, the exception, not the rule, and have survived simply as being exceptions. Seneca tells us that masters who ill-treated their slaves were pointed at in the streets,* and the tone of public opinion seems, as we said, to have been growing more humane throughout the first century. The pride of race was diminishing, and the minds of the privileged class were becoming more open to the claims of aliens and dependents. The slaves had still much to suffer, and their condition was in some respects a very miserable one, but the voice of humanity had made itself heard, and the reform, which dates from the first century, extended steadily till the evil plant was uprooted from the soil of Europe.

Humanity to criminals is generally a late product of civilisation. The Romans, however, were distinguished by the leniency of their punishments where citizens were the guilty parties. At a time when slaves might be put to a terrible death for

* Sen. de Clem. 1. 18.

the slightest offences, the gravest crime in a Roman was seldom punished except by banishment. The barbarous penalties of the Twelve Tables had long fallen into desuetude, and if we except the cruelties of some of the emperors,—the natural product of despotic power,—the Romans cannot be accused of over-severity to delinquents within their own pale A few instances might be quoted to the contrary. For example, the horrid story of the execution of the children of Sejanus displays strongly the old Roman callousness mingled with the old over-respect for legal formality. The burying alive of a Vestal by Domitian was a violent shock to the feelings of the age, though welcomed by the superstitious.

This is perhaps the best place to notice what must have been a very unpleasant feature in Roman life—namely, the brutality of bullies in the streets. If we may believe Juvenal and Apuleius,[*] the high roads and the streets of Rome were rendered unsafe for the defenceless traveller; not so much by the assaults of professional footpads, as by fashionable *roués* returning from their nocturnal revels.

[*] See also Plin. 13. 43 ; Dion. 61. 9 ; Suet. Nero 26 ; Tac. Ann. 13. 25. 47 ; with Juv. 3. 275, &c. ; Apul. Met. 2. 18.

These young blades used to patrol the streets accompanied by a gang of followers, for the purpose of insulting and beating any wayfarer who might be unfortunate enough to meet them. Their ordinary mode of procedure, according to Juvenal, was to accost the stranger in insulting language, and then fall upon with cudgels, or even swords, so that he might think himself happy if he escaped with a few teeth still in his head. Sometimes the aggressors were not content even with this, but accused their victim next day of having assaulted them. These roisterers, who went to bed in dejection if they had beaten no one that night, were often men of good position, who adopted this extraordinary means of amusing themselves. The phenomenon has not been unknown in European capitals in modern times.* Nero was the model of these " grassatores," and Otho one of his chief companions. Apuleius gives a very similar account of the state of the high-roads in the provinces. A countryman is riding on his donkey along a high road in Macedonia. A legionary soldier meets him, assaults him without any

* The " Mohocks " of the last century in London will suggest themselves as a parallel. See also Demosthenes in Cononem.

pretext, and only leaves off beating him when
he feigns to be dead. The next day he brings
a charge against the unhappy man for stealing,
and succeeds in having him led off to execution.
This is doubtless an exaggerated story, but we
have strong testimony to the existence of such
brutality to strangers and inferiors, and from
the number of references to it, it appears to have
been very common. From the point of view of
our present chapter it illustrates the evil of harsh
social distinctions, which obliterate the feelings of
social duties. It brings home to us with great
force the unpleasant position of the weak and un-
protected in Roman society, when we hear of
aggravated assaults, sometimes causing death, being
committed with impunity. The rich could defend
themselves by the help of their clients and slaves;
the poor, unless they could attach themselves to
some powerful protector, were in constant danger
of insult and outrage. To use a common modern
phrase, there was practically one law for the strong,
another for the weak.

The relief of the poor, the suffering, and the unfortunate, is another important branch of humanity.
On this point we are struck by the very large pro-

portion of the population of Rome whose fortune
or misfortune it was "aliena vivere quadra." Besides the unknown multitudes of slaves, and the
very considerable number of clients, hangers-on,
and parasites, not less than 200,000 persons were
dependent on the State for their daily food. Only
a very small minority of the inhabitants can have
paid for their own board. This fact marks a great
difference between Rome and modern cities, and
explains why "charity" there played so much
less a part than in modern times. We cannot
dignify with that honourable name the gratuitous
distribution of corn, which carried with it all the
evils of almsgiving without the advantages : like
the rest of Imperial munificence, baths, libraries,
games, &c., it was a mere political device, which
reduced indeed the want of private benevolence,
but was itself of a different nature. The same may
be said of land-distributions, which were made
occasionally in our period ; nor were the legacies
which some princes left to the people evidences
of genuine benevolence.* A movement for the

---

* We may seem here to do scant justice to the noble municipal
patriotism which left such splendid monuments of itself over the
whole empire. But this is not *humanity*, but a different virtue,
which may more fitly receive its recognition in another chapter.

D

education of poor children deserves more praise.
It was begun by Vespasian, extended by Nerva,
and carried on by his successors. Besides the
action of the State, it became common for wealthy
men to found charities in their native towns for
the free education of the poor. Pliny conferred
this benefit on the town of Comum. Hospitals
were however unknown, so far as we can tell, and
there is no trace of lunatic asylums. The insane
were not illtreated, as in England till the present
century, but were attended by ordinary physicians.
Private misfortunes were relieved by the generosity
of friends. The liberality which was often displayed in these cases is remarkable, and forms a
pleasing feature in Roman life. If a man's house
was burnt down, he was loaded with gifts of all
kinds from his neighbours, so that he might even
be a gainer by the misfortune.* The presents
might not be altogether disinterested, and the poor
man might find no one to help him in a similar
disaster, but on the whole a good deal of generosity
seems to have been practised at Rome.† When the

* Juv. 3. 222.

† Polybius indeed says, that "at Rome no one ever gives anything to anybody;" but this is hardly borne out by other evidence,
at least in our period.

amphitheatre at Fidena fell, and killed and wounded an enormous number of persons, the houses of the rich were thrown open to admit the sufferers, and surgeons and remedies supplied them free of cost.* Such instances seem to shew that "charity," though not exalted to so high a place as in Christian times, was by no means defective under the early Emperors.

The enemies of the Roman people were still treated with rigour, when occasion offered. The siege and capture of Jerusalem by Titus was perhaps the most murderous of Roman victories. On the other hand, Claudius treated the captured Caractacus with a magnanimity which had not been shewn in former days to Vercingetorix or Jugurtha. But the foreign wars of Rome in this period were comparatively few and insignificant, and we have not sufficient means of judging whether the duty of clemency to the conquered was more recognized than in the republican age.

Let us pass on for a few moments to another branch of humanity (if the word may be extended so far), namely, kindness to animals. The indifference of the southern nations of Europe to the

* Tac. Ann. 4. 63.

sufferings of animals at the present day is well
known. We may assert with confidence that
Pagan Rome was considerably in advance of modern
Italy in this respect. It would be unsafe to insist
too much on the affection of the Roman for his
pets, of which we have several curious examples;*
but we find cases of legislation, such as the ancient
law forbidding on pain of death the slaughter of
the ox,† and cases such as the capital punishment
of a child for cruelty to birds,‡ which shew how
strong was the feeling on the subject. Mr. Lecky§
quotes or refers to some interesting passages
from Ovid, Plutarch, Lucretius, and Juvenal,
illustrative ot the same feeling. We even find
persons refusing to hunt or to eat meat for conscien-
tious reasons. This pleasing feature in Roman life,
which contrasts so favourably with the practice of
many Christian nations, may be partly attributed
to the teaching of some philosophers, *e.g.* the
Pythagorean schools, which held the doctrine of

---

* For Roman pets, cf. Mart. 7. 87, where he mentions monkeys,
ichneumons, magpies, and snakes, besides the more ordinary
animals.

† This curious law was common to most of the nations of
antiquity. We find it at Athens, in Phrygia, and in other places.

‡ Quint. Instit. 5. 9.

§ History of European Morals, vol. II. p. 165.

the transmigration of souls. Stories arising from ignorance of natural history may also, as Mr. Lecky suggests, have aided to cause the conviction that the natures of men and animals are identical. We can only be surprised that no opposition was made to the cruelties of the amphitheatre.

We have deferred till now the subject which is generally the first to come into our minds when we think of Roman precept or practice in the matter of humanity. The very important part which the " games" of the amphitheatre played in the social life of Rome has been recognized by most writers on the subject. There is, probably, no feature in ancient life that appears to the modern mind more startling than that throughout the period of its highest civilisation and culture one of the main amusements of the Roman people should have been the spectacle of human bloodshed. We find it difficult to believe that men who could take pleasure in such a spectacle could have any feelings of humanity at all. We seem to be contemplating the lowest abyss to which human depravity can sink, the most hideous perversion of all the kindly sentiments of our nature.

To contemplate suffering which brings no advantage to the beholder, and to gloat over it for its own sake, may seem not an attribute of men, but of fiends. The possibility of such a moral disease has been indignantly denied by many writers on ethics, from Hobbes downwards. Selfishness, they say, may dry up the milk of human kindness, or revenge turn it to gall, but the mere sight of suffering, in the absence of such motives, can never be otherwise than painful. We believe this view to be altogether mistaken. In the happy security of our peaceful civilisation there may exist latent elements in our nature which never reveal themselves to our self-consciousness. The truth seems to be, as Professor Bain says, that this feeling is a mode of sensuous and sensual gratification, which, in the absence of countervailing sympathies, may amount to a very keen sensation of pleasure, and by habitual indulgence may produce a morbid craving of the most potent kind. In boys this tendency often shews itself; in savages it is almost universal, and produces the most hideous results; in civilised men it is generally undeveloped and scarcely felt to exist unless called out by exceptional circumstances. At Rome the gladiatorial shows afforded it the most abundant food. Even the holocausts of victims slaughtered on the sacrificial stone of the Aztec war-god must have been less demoralising to the spectators than the Roman games. The continual succession of these barbarous spectacles, the intense enthusiasm they excited, and the absence of other matters of interest which might divert the attention, kept the imagination constantly fixed on these scenes of torture and death.*

The measure of the evil wrought by the games may be taken by the neglect of the higher intellectual amusements which we observe at this period. The drama seemed tasteless and insipid to those who habitually watched the enactment of the direct tragedies in real life. The eyes that had gloated over the last contortions of human agony, the ears that had feasted themselves on the shouts and groans of mortal conflict, could never again feel much interest in the sight of blind Œdipus, or the narration of Polyxena's sacrifice.†
Even comedy had lost its charms, and could only

* Even the children played at gladiators. Epictetus M. 29. 3.

† See Tac. Dial. Or. 29, where he laments that gladiators and race-horses had left no room for noble culture.

attract when it pandered to the pruriency which shared with thirst for blood the polluted minds of the populace. The gorgeous processions which had been so popular in the republican days were now regarded with impatience.* At last even the games themselves were not sufficient to satisfy the morbid craving, unless they were varied by constant novelties in slaughter, often consisting of more wholesale bloodshed, or more horrid forms of death.†

In spite of legislative restrictions, to be referred to in another chapter, the number of victims increased, till in the reign of Trajan we read of 10,000 gladiators being exposed to fight. The combat of armed men was varied by every kind of fantastic device, appealing to the love of novelty in the spectators, which always craved for some new excitement. The combatants were armed as Thracians, as Mirmillones, as Essedarii, or as Retiarii, and especial interest was excited by a

---

* Seneca closes one of his imaginary harangues by saying, "Sed jam non sustineo vos morari. Scio quam odiosa sit circensibus pompa." Sen. Controv. 1 præf. ad fin.

† Among the most atrocious slaughters in the arena during this century may be mentioned that of the British prisoners at Rome under Claudius (Dion. 60. 30), and that of 2,500 Jews at Cæsarea in A.D. 70.

struggle between two different sorts of equipment. Even the sense of the ludicrous was appealed to by combats of blind-folded men,* of dwarfs and deformed persons,† while there are several instances on record of women descending into the arena. This last atrocity seems to have disgusted even the depraved taste of the populace, and it was eventually forbidden. The deserts of Africa and Asia were ransacked for every kind of wild beast that could be made to fight in the arena. The excitement of the spectators during the combats was intense, and shewed itself in savage shouts, such as "Habet!" "Accipe ferrum!" "Occide, ure, verbera!" "Quare tam timide incurrit in ferrum?" "Quare parum libenter moritur?"‡ By a cruel innovation the life of the vanquished gladiator was made to depend on the suffrages of the crowd, and attempts were even made to introduce games "sine missione," where no quarter was to be given. These were, however, forbidden by Augustus.§ The general practice was for the spectators to express their wishes as to the fate of the prostrate combatant by a motion of the thumb, which was

---

* Andabatœ Cic. ad Fam. 7. 10.   † Stat. Silv. 1. 57–64.
‡ Sen. Ep. 7. 4.   § Suet. Aug. 45.

turned to the breast to indicate the death thrust, or
moved downwards to signify the dropping of the
weapon.*

We have no right to wonder that this pernicious
institution was more popular than even the bull-
fights of modern Spain, and that the attraction
was so strong that even Christians in the ardour
of their newly-accepted faith often failed to tear
themselves away from the amphitheatre.† We
must admit that no element of excitement and
interest was wanting. The vast assemblage of
human beings, all intent on a common object,
was enough in itself to blunt the susceptibilities
and rouse the ardour of each individual spectator;
the magnificence and variety of the entertainment
dazzled the eye and kept the attention constantly riveted; the splendid courage with which
the combatants always faced wounds and death
took away most of the hideousness which usually
attends the violent extinction of human life; and
the spirit of partisanship, which is necessary to
identify the spectator with the scenes he wit-

* These mute gestures were often accompanied by loud shouts,
"dissono clamore," Tac. A. 1. 32.   Cf. also Suet. Cal. 30; Mart.
Spect. 29. 3; Fronto ad M. Caes. 2. 4. 4.

† Cf. Augustine, Confess. 6. 8.

nesses, was excited both by the person of the gladiator and by the method of his equipment and fighting.* When we add to these attractions the unhappy psychological phenomenon which we discussed above, we have an ample explanation of the strength of this institution, which nothing but Christianity could eradicate.

We are, however, disappointed by the tone of the cultivated classes with regard to the games. We find very few traces of the disgust which we should have expected them to arouse in a refined mind. Such as there are belong to the Empire, not to the Republic, which bears out the theory we are endeavouring to maintain, that a great awakening of humanity dates from the first century. Cicero, indeed, says that "some consider the games cruel, and possibly they are as now conducted,"† and in another place declares that he feels no pleasure in seeing a feeble man torn by a powerful beast, or a noble animal transfixed by a spear.‡ This we should expect in a man of Cicero's character, but his aversion is one of

* The rivalry between the supporters of the large and small shield was very keen in the latter half of our century.

† Tusc. 2. 17.

‡ Ep. ad Div. 7. 1.

taste and not of principle.* After the Augustan
age a slightly better tone seems to prevail.
Drusus the son of Tiberius,† and Claudius,‡ are
blamed for shewing too keen a pleasure in the
sight of bloodshed. Private writers no longer put
forward the official justification—that the sight of
strife and death promotes a military spirit in the
citizens. Literature supplies no instance of a dis-
position to gloat over the horrors of the arena ;
and Seneca condemns the games altogether, with
great eloquence and vigour,§ on the true principles of humanity. But though other indications
of awakening conscience might be quoted, the
record during the first century is on the whole
disappointing, and shews that morality had as
yet made little progress on this field. We may
now leave this painful but interesting subject,
the importance of which seemed to justify a
somewhat lengthy discussion.

* See *e.g.*, Tusc. 2. 20, where he defends the games as conducive
to courage and contempt of death.
† Tac. Ann. 1. 76.
‡ Suet. Claud.
§ Nothing could be more finely expressed than his answer to
the common plea that the sufferers were criminals. " *They* deserve to die, I know ; but what crime have *you* committed to
deserve to be a spectator of their punishment ? "

The third branch of morality which we have to discuss is that connected with the relations between the sexes. The points to be considered are: first, the extent and causes of the degradation of public morals in this particular, and, secondly, the movement of public opinion on the subject during the first century. The Romans of the early republic justly prided themselves on the purity of their domestic life, which enabled them to allow great freedom to their women, and made divorce an unknown thing. Though the legal position of the wife, as of the son, was low, women enjoyed great respect and influence, and the organism of domestic life was sound and healthy. This pleasing state of things was changed by the extension of the empire. A wave of corruption swept over Rome with the influx of Oriental wealth and Oriental slaves, the slaves especially being a fruitful source of vice, as they always are where the institution exists. The civil war, which ended with the battle of Actium, completed the dissolution of morals, and opened a period perhaps unparallelled in history for unblushing debauchery and shameless wickedness. The plague fed on its own contamination. Literature spread corruption through all classes by the audacity of its coarseness. The theatre owed its chief attraction to the manner in which it pandered to the vilest tastes. Art lent itself to depict shameless and suggestive scenes. Even religion became the ready minister of vice ; and the temples of Isis were constantly used for the vilest purposes.* The women, as is usually the case when society is thoroughly corrupt, were even more depraved than the men. Abnormal forms of vice were as common in Rome as ever in Greece. The court often set the example of the most hideous profligacy. It is unnecessary to heighten the colours of the dreadful picture by references to Juvenal, Martial, or Suetonius. It is needful to keep in mind this melancholy feature of Roman life, but no excuse is wanted for not allowing it its due proportion of space in an essay of this kind. Without further details, then, let us state that the Empire found the whole of society pervaded with the grossest immorality, that marriage was avoided to an extent which threatened the extinction of the Roman stock, that divorce was practised with a scandalous levity and fre-

* Cf. the story of Decius Mundus, in the reign of Tiberius. The strong expressions of Minucius Felix, quoted by Friedländer, shew that the evil still existed in the third century.

quency, that even military discipline and the frugality of a country life had ceased to exercise their wholesome influence on society, that religion was either silent or enlisted in the service of vice, and that belief in purity seemed to have almost vanished from the earth. It will be a more pleasing task to consider what deductions can be made from this gloomy indictment, and what hopes for the future were discernible in the darkness of Pagan wickedness.

In the first place the whole empire was not nearly so corrupt as the capital. The valley of the Po still contained a free agricultural and industrial population, whose business or simplicity preserved their virtue from contamination. The great towns of the East, such as Antioch and Alexandria, were the imitators or instructors of Rome in the worst excesses; but we would gladly believe that the western provinces, and the rural districts of the empire generally, were strangers to the worst fruits of luxury. Again, we are pleased to find that as the barbarities of the slave-owner did not quench the spirit of loyalty and fidelity in the slaves, so the laxity of morals in both sexes did not banish from society the domestic virtues of conjugal devotion. It was remarked by Velleius Paterculus* that the evil period of the civil wars was brightened by signal examples of devotion of slaves to their masters, and still more of wives to their husbands, while the bonds of filial duty seemed to have been altogether broken. And the early empire can furnish as signal examples of fidelity as the end of the republic. The courage of Porcia, the wife of Brutus, is not more admirable than the devotion of the two Arrias, mother and daughter, to their husbands.† The epitaphs of the period shew that the old ideal of womanhood was not yet extinct. Many Roman matrons, if we may trust the inscriptions on their sepulchres, still followed the simple rule of old times, " domi mansit, lanam fecit," and many were able to take the still prized title of " Univira." There is another consideration which has not been urged by other writers on the subject, but which may well make us pause before accepting too readily the pictures drawn by satirists like Juvenal, profligates like Martial, pessimists like

* Vell. 2. 67.

† Fannia, the daughter of the younger Arrias, and wife of Helvidius Priscus, shewed herself worthy of her mother and grandmother. Plin. Ep. 7. 19.

Tacitus, and scandal-mongers like Suetonius. We mean the purity and delicacy of some of the prominent writers of the age. To go back a little, as we may, Cicero, though often foul-mouthed in invective, was evidently a moral man; Virgil is conspicuous among the writers of all ages for his purity; Pliny the Younger shews all the reticence and delicacy of the modern gentleman; Seneca, Epictetus, and Plutarch urge strongly the obligation of chastity in the husband as well as the wife; and many other instances might be quoted to shew that the corruption was not by any means universal. These are the chief arguments we can find to oppose to the fearful array of evidence against the morality of Imperial Rome. It must be confessed that they make but a poor show. We may hope that civilization will never again sink into so deep a degradation.

It remains to consider whether in this as in other branches of morality, the first century kindled the life-giving spark which was to burn so brightly afterwards. We have just mentioned the noble teaching of Seneca and Plutarch on the duty of chastity. Still more Christian in

E

tone are the precepts of Musonius Rufus, who condemned all illicit intercourse either in or out of wedlock, and taught that " the virtues of men and women are the same." This, which had never been inculcated by the older Stoics, seems a forecast of the ascetic notion of purity which was developed by Christianity. We find many instances of it in the next century outside the pale of Christianity, but scarcely any other indications of it in our period.* We do, however, trace some desire for moral reform in this as in other respects towards the close of the century. It never reached boiling point, but "simmered gently on the surface of society,"† and did something to check the extravagance and ostentation of vice which is so painful a feature of the age.

We purpose to conclude this chapter by a few remarks on what we have learnt to call the sanctity of human life, as understood at Rome.

---

* Epictetus, however, regards celibacy as a higher state than marriage. This view, which was held by nearly all early Christian writers, is quite contrary to the ordinary ideas of antiquity, and can only be due to the *ascetic* notion of the relations between the sexes.

† Merivale.

The attitude of society towards murder, infanticide, and homicide generally, and the kindred question of suicide, presents some points of interest which should not be passed over. To take first the question of murder of adult free persons. There is much evidence to prove that domestic crime was extremely common in this century. Parricide, perhaps the most unnatural crime of all, is noticed as increasing in frequency. In earlier times there had been no legislation on the subject, the crime being regarded as too horrible to be committed. Poisoning of husbands and wives was apparently carried on to a frightful extent. We need only refer to the awful revelation of wickedness in Cicero's speech pro Cluentio, and to Martial's half-humorous denunciations, *e.g.*, Ep. 9, 15 :

> " Inscripsit tumulis septem scelerata virorum
> ' Se fecisse ' Chloe ; quid pote simplicius ? "

the literal truth of which may be doubted, but this does not affect their value as evidence. Professional poisoners, such as Locusta, found plenty of occupation at court and among the upper classes. The chief motives of these crimes were love of money and adulterous passion, especially the former. We have before mentioned the baneful result of combined luxury and idleness on the morals of the aristocracy. A ruined man of fashion, or a member of a fallen family, had no means of repairing his fortunes except by legacy-hunting or marrying an heiress, and the temptation to crime in the frantic pursuit of wealth was often irresistible. Murders by the criminal classes, in housebreaking or highway robbery, are sometimes mentioned. Assassination, such as was common in Italy in the 15th century, was never a Roman crime. The duel, that strangest product of Christian civilization, was absolutely unknown. It was characteristic of the Roman temperament to discourage personal violence in redressing private wrongs, and to employ legal remedies to settle even " affairs of honour." At Rome, as in England, slander was confuted and punished not at the sword's point, but by the verdict of a court of justice. The ordinary course of a quarrel in high life at Rome was dignified and temperate. Germanicus sends Piso a cartel—not of challenge to mortal combat, but to inform him that their acquaintance and friendship must cease.* Tiberius

* Tac. Ann. 2. 70, and 3. 12.

sends a similar message to Labeo.* Even a wager at law was employed in cases of this kind. The case of slaves has already been dealt with.

To take next the cases of abortion and infanticide. The former it appears was not discouraged by law, and was very extensively practised. The art was a regular part of the physician's practice, and was apparently well understood.† We find praises of women for not resorting to it. The destruction of a new-born infant was according to some authorities forbidden by law, but it was certainly common.‡ Parents whose sense of pity prevented them from killing an infant, often exposed it, in which case it either died of neglect or was reared as a slave or prostitute by persons who made a trade of the practice. The habit of "limiting the number of children," as Tacitus euphemistically calls it, was condemned on political grounds as tending to diminish population at a time when the human harvest was bad ; but we do

* Tac. Ann. 6. 29. The emperor, however, speaks of "reviving an old custom," so perhaps the formality was nearly obsolete in our period.

† See, however, Ovid. "Saepe suos utero quae necat ipsa perit."

‡ See Sen. de Ira. 1. 15. 2. "Liberos quoque, si debiles monstrosique editi sunt, *mergimus.*"

not find the moral condemnation which modern society passes on the practice, a judgment which is due to a new conception of the guilt of homicide, introduced by Christianity. The practice of infanticide was certainly highly mischievous at Rome in this period, and contributed not a little to the gradual extinction of the Roman race.

The kindred subject of suicide holds an extremely prominent place in Roman social history, especially in our period. At no other time probably has deliberate withdrawal from life been so common as under the early empire at Rome. Men committed suicide to escape the pains of mortal disease, or to anticipate condemnation for crime; many resolved to end their life when they felt old age coming upon them; some even determined to accompany a beloved person to the tomb. The resolution was carried out with a calm deliberation which distinguishes Roman suicides from the rash and sudden acts of self-destruction with which we are familiar. We read of men calmly waiting the verdict of their physicians on their chances of recovery from sickness, before deciding whether to live or die; of others fixing a day to end their lives, and notifying it to their relations; of others choosing a lingering

form of death, apparently with the object of dying
in the presence of their friends. Some noble men
put an end to their lives in despair of their country,
under the vile tyranny of some of the emperors;
one man, on the other hand, postponed his death
till after the assassination of Domitian, that he
might die free. Public opinion was generally
favourable to suicide. Many philosophers, it is
true, condemned it as a desertion of one's post, but
the general feeling was, that it was an open door
through which man might escape at any time from
the woes of life, and that he had a perfect right to
avail themselves of it. The best indication of the
Roman view of the subject is that given by Pliny,[*]
when he says, "There are some things that even
God cannot do; for he cannot seek death if he
wishes it—that best of gifts which he has given to
men amid all the miseries of life." Seneca, in a
burst of brilliant eloquence, enumerates the sufferings from which death makes us free, and con-
gratulates the human race on the liberty which is
thus within their reach.[†] Many distinguished
Romans, Musonius Rufus, Silius Italicus, Petronius,

---

[*] Plin. H. N. 2. 5.
[†] Sen. Cons. ad Marciam, 20.

Otho the Emperor * among them, put into practice
the precepts of philosophers. The death of Cato
became a commonplace of panegyric. Regular
epidemics of suicides appeared in various places.
A law had to be made preventing accused persons
saving their property for their families by antici-
pating their sentence. The idea of life being sacred
in itself was quite foreign to the Roman mind.
Moralists condemned suicide, when they did so, as
desertion or cowardice, but not as murder. The
legislature did not interfere in the matter, and
philosophers were left to discuss the subject calmly
and impartially. As we have seen, they were
divided on the question, but the hardness of the
Roman temperament predisposed men to regard
life very lightly, and the arguments from patriotism
and personal dignity did not appeal to the many.
Where a materialistic view of life prevails, suicide
is naturally looked upon as reasonable in certain
cases, and is likely to be common, especially among
the educated, who are more influenced by general
ideas. Christianity has certainly increased the
seriousness with which death is regarded, and this

* Other suicides in the first century were Cocceius Nerva, under
Tiberius, Sextius Severus, Albucius Silus, Corellius Rufus, and
Titius Aristo.

fact makes it rather difficult for us to enter into the feelings of the ancients on the subject.

We have now concluded our brief survey of the state of pagan morality at Rome during the first century. It is in most respects a dark picture, though some writers have painted it in yet blacker colours. But the dictates alike of feeling and of reason forbid us to believe the worst accounts that have reached us. It is no disparagement of the work wrought by Christianity to hesitate before accepting evidence which would argue a radical change in human nature. We should rather rest assured that in the worst times virtue has never left the earth, and that in its broad features human nature is the same for good and evil as it was 2,000 years ago. The testimony of an age against itself is always overdrawn. Let us correct the fierce invective of Juvenal by the wise warning of Seneca.*
" We must guard against letting blame fall on our own age. This has always been the complaint of our ancestors, that manners have been corrupted, that vice reigns, that human life is deteriorating and falling into every kind of wickedness. We lament in the same strain, and our descendants

* De Ben. 1. 10.

will do the same after us. In reality, however, those things do not change, but only fluctuate slightly at times like the ebb and flow of the sea ; now one vice prevails most, now another, but bad men have always existed, and (alas!) always will." " Morality, like everything else," says Tacitus, " moves round in a circle."* We in the nineteenth century have accustomed ourselves to look for and expect some progress, but we must at least try to avoid the temptation to blacken our ancestors that we may make our own improvement seem the greater.

* Tac. Ann. 3. 55.

CHAPTER IV.

THE GOVERNMENT AND SOCIETY.

IT is not possible to draw a sharp dividing line between political and social history. It is true that the ordinary current of daily life seems to flow on almost independent of political changes. Here and there the career of individuals or even the position of classes may be altered, but after all the greater part of our lives is free from the influence of government, whether it be republican or despotic. Still there are ways in which the form of government materially affects social life, and in which a violent change in the constitution may be expected to modify the character of a country's civilization. It is a matter of great importance whether speech is free or not, whether a man may in word and with the pen "speak the thing he will": whether he is unfettered in the exercise of his religion and the prosecution of his speculations: and whether in the education of his children he may use his own discretion as to the subjects taught and the maxims inculcated. Again, it is a matter of importance whether each individual feels himself a sharer in the government, or whether he regards himself merely as a subject, with no voice in the making of the laws which he has to obey. It is important whether the laws are equal to all classes, and whether the citizen has an open career before him if his abilities enable him to rise. All these matters do affect the social life of a nation, though they belong in themselves to politics ; and for this reason a short chapter on the social aspect of Roman Imperialism seems to be called for.

The Homeric attribute of kings was " shepherds of the people." The expression sounds genial and pleasant, but the converse is less satisfactory. A nation of civilized men should not be comparable to sheep in a sheepfold. A sheepfold may be a model of order and good government, but its members being without responsibility may be without intelligence. A community organized on this principle is rightly regarded as a low type of state. To a great extent this misfortune had befallen Rome in the loss of her freedom. The emperor was now the visible embodiment of the constitution, and the fountain of all public movement of every kind. The tendency to centralization became so strong that nothing could be done without communicating with Rome. The machinery of the State seemed complete without the interference of private persons : there was now no place for the citizen soldier or for the independent republican magistrate. As a consequence, the feeling of citizenship was largely impaired. The Roman felt himself no longer a citizen but a subject, a difference by no means unimportant.

The despotism of the Cæsars was not intrusive, partly because it was so strong. The military force on which it chiefly depended was generally kept away at the frontiers, and Rome was not annoyed by the presence of a repressive police. We do not hear of *contiones* being forbidden or dispersed, and the *collegia* or clubs, though not held in much favour, maintained their existence and increased in number and influence. Thought and speech were generally free, though with exceptions. To take first the matter of education. We are surprised to find the absolute freedom of subjects which was allowed to teachers. The praises of tyrannicide were a common stock-subject for declamation, and the burning questions of past history were handled with equal freedom. The only occasions, so far as we know, on which this liberty was violated, were the banishment of Carrinas Secundus by Caligula for declaiming against tyrants, the execution of Curiatius Maternus by Domitian for the same offence, and that of Musonius and Virginius by Nero. Literature was more checked.* Good emperors, of course, allowed more freedom than tyrants, but taking the century as a whole, the fear of offending the government, or the desire of conciliating it, has an evil influence on both poetry and prose. Instances of punishments inflicted on writers are not rare; the fate of Lutorius Priscus, under Tiberius, and of Arulenus Rusticus and Herennius Senecio, under Domitian, are cases in point. With regard to religion, the government was very tolerant. No compulsion was exercised to make men conform to the State religion; the utmost latitude of thought and practice prevailed without hindrance. The only exceptions were in the case of those religions which were aggressively hostile to polytheism, and represented a national and disloyal

* We shall speak of this more fully in another chapter.

spirit, like that of the Jews, or those which were
regarded as immoral or grossly superstitious, like
some imported from Asia Minor and the far East.
There was, however, one important point connected
with this subject in which the empire allowed no
heterodoxy. The worship of the genius of the
emperor is one of the most curious features of the
century. It is most difficult for us to put ourselves
in the frame of mind in which such a worship
seems possible. We must not, however, regard it
as merely a political device or an extravagance of
tyranny, for it was clearly much more. No doubt
fear and sycophancy played an important part
in the divine honours paid to the emperors, but
there was a substratum of genuine feeling among
many of the worshippers. That this was the case
cannot be doubted by any who have observed the
numerous notices of the subject in the literature of
the time. What then was the feeling which
prompted so extraordinary a manifestation? Was
it akin to the honours paid to the heroes and demigods of mythology? In part perhaps it was: but
we must remember that these heroes were sanc-
tified by antiquity, and exalted by venerable
tradition, while the imperial "gods" actually owed

their apotheosis to a vote of the senate, or the
filial piety of their successors. It appears certain
that some emperors never were deified, and that
their images could accordingly be profaned without
sacrilege or treason. Deification was thus, at
best, the favourable verdict of a prince's successor
and subjects on his character. It was not customary to worship an emperor exactly as a god
during his lifetime, at least at Rome. Courtiers
generally spoke of the emperor as " *our* god,"
" Namque erit ille *mihi* semper deus," " præsens
divus *habebitur* Augustus," which does not quite
put him on a level with Jupiter and Apollo. The
decent limitation was, however, less and less
observed as the century wore on. In the provinces temples were erected to living emperors by
the score, and every token of divine homage was
rendered to them. At last Domitian threw off all
disguise, and encouraged his courtiers to give him
the title of " lord and god." We must remember
that these extravagances were not new. The poor
oppressed provincials of the east had long been
accustomed to propitiate their governors by quasi-
divine honours, and we can easily understand how
under the empire the degrading practice of servility

extended itself even to Rome. But other reasons probably aided the growth of the custom. The man who ruled with absolute power the whole of the known civilised world must have seemed almost superhuman ; it was almost pardonable to regard him with the awe inspired by a divine being. And not only was his person exalted above the rest of mankind, and his power terrible in its extent and strength, but he stood forth as the representative of that mighty empire, the like of which the world had never seen, and which was now for the first time concentrated under the sceptre of a single man. The senate was no longer an assembly of kings, the Roman people was no longer an army of generals, but the empire was there, more imposing than ever in its wide extent and its new tranquillity, and the emperor was the living embodiment of its strength and its genius. The worship of Rome had really been the foundation of the Roman's faith from the first ; and to some extent the emperor inherited what was left of the pious devotion. But whatever was the origin of the worship, it was enforced with atrocious jealousy by the legislation of the time. Men were never safe against accusations brought

F

by professional informers of having insulted the
image of an emperor. Even coins bearing the
deified features were to be regarded as sacred; and
slaves could find an asylum from the lash of an
infuriated master by taking refuge in the vicinity
of an imperial statue. To the ordinary citizen
this part of the law of *majestas* must have been
the most galling part of the yoke imposed by the
despotism.

Private conversation on politics was made unsafe by the machinations of the informers. It was
considered best to avoid hazardous subjects in
social gatherings, and specially when wine might
throw the guests off their guard. This, of course,
differed at different periods in the century. Some
emperors discouraged the *delatores,* and allowed
their subjects to speak on any subject with freedom, while others had spies in every house, and
noted every word with jealous tyranny. It is
more remarkable that in certain particulars the
Roman populace were able to maintain unimpaired
their right of free speech. We shall mention here-
after the "license" of the amphitheatre and the
circus, where the people were wont to clamour for
anything they wanted, including the punishment

of unpopular ministers; and the telling allusions
so frequent in the theatre, which were caught up
readily by the audience. Another characteristic
privilege was that of *pasquinade*, a truly Roman
invention. Even Nero tolerated the most offensive
and cutting epigrams against his crimes. After
he had murdered his mother, the streets of Rome
were placarded with the following witty couplet:

"Quis neget Æneæ clara de stirpe Neronem?
Sustulit hic matrem, sustulit ille patrem;"

and Tiberius had to endure the transformation of
his name into "Biberius Caldius Mero." The most
abominable accusations were freely made against
any unpopular ruler, and many of them have found
their way into the scurrilous work of Suetonius.
Romans still valued their "simplicity" and "ur-
banity" of speech, words which were often
euphemisms for hideous grossness and brutal jesting.
The license thus allowed them seems, however, to
deserve mention as a characteristic feature of the
time.

We see, then, that the despotism of the Cæsars,
though in some respects mild and liberal in its
character, was in others sufficiently galling and
intrusive to exercise a malign influence on society.

F 2

This influence is perceptible in the *unreality* which seems to pervade the life of the period. Both in daily habits and in literature men seem to be constantly straining after effect, and thinking anxiously how they appear to others. Rome seems to be a kind of stage, on which the citizens perform their part, as they wish others to see them ; but it is all acting, not genuine living. Affectation and hypocrisy reign supreme. Everyone tries to hide his own nature, and appear something else. The noblest spirits are a prey to vanity, and angle for compliments from their friends. Added to this, a general feeling of insecurity and distrust pervades the intercourse of society and checks the free development both of friendship and of genius. This paralysis of true healthy life was the price paid by Rome for the loss of her freedom, a loss which to the superficial observer seemed more than compensated by the termination of anarchy and the establishment of settled order.

It will not be digressing much to consider how Roman society came to acquiesce in the loss of liberty consequent on the change of constitution, how it probably regarded its position, and what compensations it could enjoy.

In the first place,* the restoration of peace and
order must have been felt as an immense boon.
Rome was no longer torn by intestine strife, to
the delight of Parthians and Germans. Once more
she could turn her attention to foreign conquest,
still the passion of all patriots. "The accursed
civil wars had arrested the progress of the legions,
which might ere now have subdued Bactria, and
carried the fasces beyond the Indus. Now the
victorious eagles will penetrate to Thule and Cale-
donia, and palm-bearing Idume. There still remain
new lands to conquer. Babylon does not yet pay
tribute ; the Arabs and Seres are not yet our sup-
pliants ; the Indian laurel has yet to be placed in
the lap of Jove." Such is the language of Silius
and Statius. From this point of view even patriots
might regard the empire as a blessing : it certainly
for the time increased the aggressive power of
Rome, though a wise policy restrained conquest
within narrow limits. In fact, security was much
more important than glory, as Augustus felt. His
passionate distress at the defeat of Varus was
caused by his consciousness that the justification
of the empire really rested in its power to ward

* See Tac. Ann. 1, 2, on this subject.

off foreign attack, and preserve security at home.
The "Pax Romana" was the great gift of Cæsarism
to the world.

We should also notice the republican avoidance
of titles and court etiquette which signalised the
early despotism. The person of the emperor was
always accessible : he mixed in ordinary society at
banquets and entertainments : he corresponded
with his officials in a tone of easy familiarity, as
we see in the letters between Pliny and Trajan :
and he never claimed either from subjects or aliens
the insignia of royalty. When the king of Parthia
began a despatch, "Arsaces, king of kings, to Fla-
vius Vespasianus, greeting," that emperor replied
in the same form, disdaining to notice the arrogance of the Oriental sultan.

But the idea of subjection to a master could not
really shock the minds of Romans at this period.
They were too much used to a society organised
on this principle. The existence of the slave world
was a standing contradiction of the rights of man,
and furnished examples and lessons in servility
which the masters were not slow to learn. The
idea of domination and subjection as the natural
order of things had really penetrated the spirit of

the age, and choked all remaining aspirations after liberty. With what satisfaction Statius enunciates his theory of universal servitude !

> " Quid enim terrisque poloque
> Parendi sine lege manet ?   Vice cuncta reguntur,
> Alternisque regunt : propriis sub regibus omnis
> Terra ; premit felix regum diademata Roma :
> Hanc ducibus frenare datum : mox crescit in illos
> Imperium superis."

We seem not far from Claudian's " magnorum suboles regum " addressed to an empress. The malign influence of slavery was felt by the Romans themselves. " You are indignant," says Seneca to his countrymen, " if your slave or freedman or client dares to answer you again ; and then you complain that the liberty which you have destroyed at home has been taken from the Republic."* A remarkable passage, which indicates with true discrimination the source of the diseases of the body politic.

In reality the inhabitants of the Roman empire were fitting themselves rapidly for their destiny as subjects of an autocrat. We need not expatiate on the disintegration of nationalities and the cosmopolitan feelings which were growing throughout

* Sen. de Ira 3. 35.

the century. The old narrow patriotism, which
was the safeguard of political freedom, was fast
disappearing, and men began to pride themselves
on being citizens of the world, which in all times
has been a pretext for selfish individualism. The
opening out of the world to trade and travel, was,
however, a quite legitimate ground of satisfaction.
It was a real benefit conferred by the empire, and
one that was highly appreciated. The loss of liberty,
and of the feelings which liberty fosters, was a misfortune for which nothing could make up ; but the
enlargement of sympathies, and opening of the
mind consequent on the fusion of nationalities,
were no small compensation. Never before in the
history of the world (shall we add, never since ?)
had the nations of the civilised world been brought
so near each other. Commerce was secured, and
flourished under a widely extended system of free
trade ; brigandage and piracy were suppressed, for
the first time since men began to float ships in the
Mediterranean ; order and prosperity seemed to
be established over the whole empire. Never till
the present century has travel been so easy or so
frequent ; every one who had money and leisure
might visit securely the historical scenes of an-

tiquity, the masterpieces of nature's handiwork, or the last conquests of civilization; one language, one system of coinage, carried the traveller over lands where now all is local and different, and all these blessings were the gift of the Eternal City, which seemed no longer the mistress but the mother of the world.

> " Hæc est, in gremium victos quæ sola recepit,
> Humanumque genus communi nomine fovit
> Matris non dominæ ritu ; civesque vocavit
> Quos domuit, nexuque pio longinqua revinxit :
> Hujus pacificis debemus moribus omnes
> Quod veluti patriis regionibus utitur hospes ;
> Quod sedem mutare licet ; quod cernere Thulen
> Lusus, et horrendos quondam penetrare recessus ;
> Quod bibimus passim Rhodanum, potamus Oronten,
> Quod cuncti gens una sumus."*

The provincials gained also in better administration. This was, in great measure, the consequence of the more liberal feelings which, as we said, were growing up under the empire. It was natural that as the exclusiveness of nationality diminished, a more generous treatment of subjects and aliens was promoted. Some have denied that

* Claudian de Cons. Stilich. 3. 150–159.

this was the case;* but the evidence for the improvement is very strong. Even such men as Petronius and Vitellius were clean-handed as governors of provinces, and the testimony of contemporary writers, Philo, Josephus, Strabo, Plutarch, and others, is all in favour of the belief that extortion and oppression were rarer than under the republic. Even the frequency of trials for maladministration is, if rightly considered, a proof of the vigilance of the central government in the interest of the provinces.

Another pleasing feature in this connection is the encouragement and practice of what we may call municipal patriotism. It is a side of Roman life which fairly belongs to our subject. We hear frequently of grants from the treasury to aid sufferers from accidents. Thus six millions of sesterces were given to Lugdunum after a fire in the year 65;† ten millions in 53 to Bononia.‡ Augustus and Vespasian both practised the same munificence on

---

* On this side may be mentioned the picture drawn by Juvenal 8. 87–139; the cases of Valerius Messalla in Asia, under Augustus, of Silius in Germany, of Piso in Spain, and of Felix and Pontius Pilate in Judæa. The evidence on the other side is, however, much stronger.

† Tac. Ann. 16. 13.

‡ Tac. Ann. 12. 58.

several occasions. The early emperors did not build much in provincial towns except by way of indemnity for accident, but they encouraged private citizens to erect public buildings in their native towns, and the practice became very common. We recognise, with pleasure, some remains of the old patriotism surviving in this shape. Rich men took a pride in embellishing their own towns with baths, libraries, temples, and other public buildings. Endowments for education, or the relief of the destitute, became common, and even small country towns often enjoyed these advantages through the liberality of their citizens.

Such acts of munificence must have been a poor substitute for genuine patriotism, but it may be doubted whether many felt the deprivation. For the generality of Rome's subjects and citizens in the first century the empire must have seemed a desirable institution, which enabled them to satisfy most of their wants, and live in comparative comfort and security. Material prosperity is always the main thing with the mass of mankind; and those nobler sentiments which sometimes lead men to rise above it were, as we have said, scarcely possible in the first century. The intellectual voluptuary who represented the upper class at Rome found himself quite in his element; and those who had to work for their living, so far as their position was altered, found more security and better chances of profit and success than in the disordered times of the Republic. Regrets and discontent were chiefly confined to the philosophers, a class, morally important, but numerically insignificant, whose exalted theories raised them above content in ease and indolence, and revealed to them the true significance of the empire of the Cæsars.

CHAPTER V.

LITERATURE AND ART.

THE victory of Augustus was probably a misfortune for Roman literature, though few would have predicted a decline while that brilliant company of poets and historians flourished under the Imperial patronage of the second Cæsar. But though the immediate results of the Empire were splendid, the cramping and paralysing influence of despotism was not long in making itself felt. It acted in three ways. First, it obliged writers to spoil their work and do violence to their conscience by direct flattery to the reigning emperor. This was carried to a monstrous extent, and was practised even by the most honourable men. Next the loss of free speech corrupted the intellectual honesty and manly straightforwardness of the community. Men ceased to be their real selves, and to speak their real sentiments, even when no danger threatened them. The literature of our period is pervaded by affectation, hollow rhetoric, and a constant straining after effect. Words, not things, were the first object with poet and prose writer alike: men cared less to say what was true and of sterling worth than to gain a transitory reputation by following the shallow taste of the day. Again, despotism influenced the proportion of the kinds of composition. Poetry gained at the expense of prose; history, which was a very congenial pursuit to the Romans of the Republic, became very dangerous, and we have suffered by the discouragement thus given to historians, as well as by the trammels which fettered those who did venture to write. In the reign of Tiberius, Titus Labienus, while reading his history to his friends, turned over several pages, with the remark " These will be read after my death." His caution, however, did not save him, for his book was confiscated and burnt. A stronger instance is that of Cremutius Cordus, who was actually accused and driven to suicide for calling Cassius "the last of the Romans." His book was also burnt, but copies of it were hidden and afterwards published. We can only be surprised that such tyranny did not ruin literature altogether. Happily the better emperors allowed much more freedom, and the worst tyrants were not suffered to reign till the natural end of their lives. Still, the mischief done to history was great, as Tacitus himself confesses. Facts were suppressed or falsified during an emperor's lifetime, and exaggerated through hatred after his death.

Another cause of the unreality of Roman literature at this epoch is to be found in the system of education. Declamation and poetry formed the staple subjects, and poetry was chiefly taught as an aid to declamation. The pupil was instructed in composing themes on given subjects, sometimes delivering a harangue to an imaginary jury, sometimes writing an essay to prove a given proposition, sometimes arguing with another pupil in the presence of the instructor, as used to be done at Cambridge. Questions of casuistry were often chosen, the pupil, of course, taking the side assigned him by the teacher. This system was only too well calculated to develope the tendency of the age to affectation, unreality, and empty declamation. We see the fruits of it as well in Lucan as in Seneca, in Statius as in Velleius.

We may also notice the evil effect of the "cacoethes scribendi" which had come upon the Roman

people. We find various artifices obviously employed to catch the popular ear, which else might
have failed to notice the work in the multitudinous
buzz of poetasters and rhetoricians. The means
employed are those with which we are so painfully
familiar in the nineteenth century. One writer
tries to let off a perpetual fire of squibs or epigrams : another daubs on his colours to be seen a
mile off: another plays bold tricks with syntax
and construction : a fourth enwraps himself in
mystifying obscurity. All endeavour to be *striking*
in one way or another, and, of course, all fail to
retain the grace and dignity of true genius.

It is time, however, to specify more accurately
the literary movements of the century. The
ordinary division into the Julian and Flavian eras
is no arbitrary one, but a real coincidence. The
accession of Vespasian, so important a landmark
in other branches of our subject, is equally so as
the beginning of a reaction in literature against the
fashions of the last half century. It is to this
earlier division that our remarks above mainly
apply. The reign of Tiberius exemplifies the
deadening weight with which tyranny can oppress
literature. As the brilliant names of the Augustan

era disappear, a dull blank succeeds. All seems under a cloud. Perhaps the shadow of the great names had a depressing effect as well as the jealousy of the Emperor. Then under Claudius the copious stream of silver age literature bursts forth with all its transient vivacity. The characteristics of the age are a feverish extravagance and unrestrained violence of expression. It is the saturnalia of the declaimer. History is represented by two works published before the death of Tiberius, the servile and affected book of Velleius, and the feeble and rhetorical anecdotes of Valerius Maximus. Seneca, the noblest figure of the age, extorts our admiration by his steady perception of objective or abstract morality, and by his philanthropic desire to improve his fellow men, in both of which points he marks a real advance in the moral theory of his age. He has not, however, escaped the vicious style of his contemporaries. He is declamatory, epigrammatic, jerky, sometimes unreal in tone. We cannot deny the truth of Quintilian's criticism that he sacrificed true excellence of style to gain the applause of the vulgar. In Lucan, the representative of the age in poetry, the same faults appear most clearly. His

epic is a string of declamations, the intervening
narrative (often really the most important) is
hurried over whenever it does not lend itself to his
rhetoric ; and so the proportion and even the in-
telligibility of the poem is seriously impaired. The
violent exaggeration of the descriptions offends our
taste as much as the affectation of learning ; and
the poet shews an evident relish for detailed scenes
of torture and bloodshed, which suggests that he or
his patrons were deeply corrupted in their taste by
the horrors of the amphitheatre. His flattery of
Nero, though nauseous enough, is perhaps excu-
sable. These writers, though vastly inferior to
their predecessors of the time of Augustus, have
yet to some extent the merit of originality. They
were not conscious of their defects, and therefore
disdained to borrow their style or their matter
from those who had gone before them. Lucan
seldom imitates Virgil ; Seneca owes little to Cicero.
Petronius may even claim the merit of attaining
excellence in an almost new branch of literature.
For a few years Rome was satisfied with the new
development ; but its faults were too apparent
to escape detection for long ; and with the death
of Nero the inevitable reaction set in.

"Scripsit majore cura quam ingenio" is Pliny's criticism on Silius Italicus, and this, as Merivale says, may be taken as the motto of the Flavian era. A strong reaction now set in against the school of Lucan and Seneca, and men began to turn with pleasure to the nobler works of the Augustan age. The affectation and unreality which had been growing during the last fifty years had now become really intolerable; there was no remedy except in conscious imitation of better models. Accordingly the poets of this period, Statius and Silius, are close, though not servile, imitators of Virgil; they lack the vigour of Lucan, but avoid his worst faults. It cannot be said, however, that they impress us with their *reality*. Statius gives us a constant succession of pretty word-paintings, composed rather with a view to the recitation-hall than to satisfy the student of the "Thebaid" as a whole. It is "*ars*," not "*in-genium*," throughout; he is never dull, but never inspiring or inspired. This elaboration of parts at the expense of the whole is characteristic of the autumn of a literature; the influence of recitations is peculiar to Rome, but not characteristic of this era. On the contrary, most of the Flavian literature was obviously meant to be *read*, not recited. In fact, the eternal recitations had become such a nuisance that the public began to strike against them. Martial describes the poet with his manuscript as more formidable than a tigress robbed of her whelps. The cheapness of books made the system really useless,* and only the laziness of the public, and, perhaps, the crabbed writing of the manuscripts, had allowed recitation to flourish as long as it did. Silius is an agreeable but not a very powerful writer. His epic is tolerably well arranged, and contains few faults of taste. Both he and Statius are sobriety itself compared with Lucan.

There are indications that the material condition of the poet had not changed for the better since the Julian era. Some poets (*e.g.* Silius) were rich men, and free from anxiety of this kind; but Martial is perpetually begging for money from the emperor and from his friends, and he does not seem to have got anything from Domitian, in spite of his servility. Martial shews us other annoyances of the poet's life: the unscrupulous pla-

* We should notice also the increase of public libraries about this time. Eventually Rome contained no less than 28 of these institutions.

giarism of bad writers, and their equally dishonest habit of fathering their own productions upon a great name. Again, the jealousy of literary men shews itself disagreeably. Martial seems to have had a chronic quarrel with Statius. On the other hand, Pliny the Younger seems to have been on the pleasantest terms with his literary contemporaries.

Martial is the most brilliant representative of the Flavian era. His epigrams are absolutely perfect of their kind, and have never been surpassed or even rivalled. The obscenity which disfigures them is an evil sign of the times, but it was considered a necessary adjunct of that kind of poetry. Even the virtuous and refined Pliny composed some very improper epigrams, which have come down to us. Martial, however, carried it to excess, in his thirst for popularity and patronage. His servility is hardly less offensive than his indecency. In this, however, he was rivalled by Statius, who did not grudge his incense to the freedmen Etruscus aud Abascantus.

Juvenal in some respects belongs to the age before him. His ideas are old-fashioned, reflecting the hardness and exclusivenes of the ancient

Roman character, which was now so fast disappearing. His invectives against the Greeks, his
hatred of parvenus, his coarse ferocity in dealing
with the female sex, are all part of this retro-
spective tendency. He left no successor and no
imitator in the second century.

To turn to the prose of the Flavian era. The
leader and mouthpiece of the reaction is Quintilian.
He metes out much less than justice to Seneca and
his school, and is never tired of setting up Cicero
as the canon of good taste and good style. His
own work is admirable, of its kind; clear, thoughtful,
and temperate. His criticisms are all worthy of
attention, and are delivered without affectation or
bombast.

The graver tone of the age was reflected in its
histories. The old conception of the historian, as
an artist in prose, whose pictures were founded,
indeed, on real events, but were avowedly embel-
lished for the pleasure of his readers, was no longer
deemed sufficient. In Tacitus we have a historian
of the modern kind; a man with a mission and a
purpose, who is terribly in earnest with his facts
and theories. In spite of the crippling influence of
tyranny, which no doubt thinned the ranks of

historians, we welcome one name, at least, of the highest genius in this difficult time.

The industry of the aristocratic student is well typified in the elder Pliny, whose habits we have already described. His work is an undigested congeries of facts, the sweepings of a hundred note books, which do not derive any of their value from the medium through which they have been transmitted to posterity. His nephew is a more interesting character. His letters have been well described as giving us our best picture of the Roman gentleman. The expression aptly denotes the character of the man as he has drawn it for us himself. No other work of Roman literature gives us so high an idea of the real *civilisation* of the age as Pliny's letters. They show a refinement of ideas and true culture which are not apparent in his contemporaries, and they are thus a valuable corrective of the common tendency to brand Roman civilisation as only material and external. In most ways Pliny is nearer the nineteenth century than any writer of the middle ages. His tastes, sympathies, and even modes of expression, are strangely modern. Now he describes the beauties of nature with a fine appreciation; now he interests himself in founding

a school and free library at his native town; now
he writes a letter of condolence or of recommenda-
tion; now he shews graceful consideration for
his dependents. All is amazingly modern—rather
French than English in its vanity and want of
reserve, but nearer to us than the English writings
of the time of Elizabeth.

It remains to notice the reaction in favour of
the ante-Augustan poets which took place in the
early empire. Even the great Augustan poets
themselves were attacked for disparaging criticism
of Lucilius and Ennius. But the new style at first
carried all before it. The archaic school comes
into prominence in the last half of the century, and
grows in strength till it culminates about the time
of the Antonines. In our period it had not yet
gained its victory. Horace and Virgil were not
yet displaced by Nævius and Ennius; Cicero still
held the field against Caius Gracchus and Cato.
But the tendency to neglect the moderns was
increasing all the time. It was a sign that the
nation was losing its taste, and felt that it was
losing it. The rugged efforts of the founders of
Latin poetry were admired not for themselves,
but as being free from the false accretions of later

times. Men could not even venture to set up the Augustans as models, for fear of imbibing the first beginnings of decadence. The only safe course seemed to be to go back as far as possible, and worry the minds of schoolboys with the uncouth and obsolete phrases of the third and second centuries, B.C., which, at least, no one could accuse of meretricious ornament or emasculate smoothness. We notice even in the mature writings of the silver age the reappearance of several words which had passed out of use for a hundred years, doubtless the result of this fashion in education.

In the fine arts, sculpture, painting, and music, Rome fully acknowledged her inferiority to Greece, and proudly disdained to compete with her. The well-known lines of Virgil—

> " Excudent alii spirantia mollius æra
> Credo equidem, et vivos ducent de marmore vultus ;
> Tu regere imperio populos, Romane, memento,"

are a faithful expression of Roman feeling on the subject. Art was beneath the dignity of the conquerors of the world. The most ardent patriotism need not blush to confess inferiority in the use of the chisel or the paint-brush. But in truth it was not only pride but conscious inability that pre-

vented Italy from entering the field in art-compe-
tition with Greece. For many generations Rome
had been full of the masterpieces of Phidias, Poly-
cletus, Apelles, and Mentor, but no Roman school
of sculpture or painting was brought into being by
the presence of these works of genius. No books
on art from a Roman pen called the attention of
citizens to the special beauties of each artist ; no
real appreciation of art is shewn even by the cultivated poets of the first century. The raptures of
Statius over a grand collection or an imposing
building are not those of the artist ; the Augustan
poets scarcely mention the "nation of statues"
that adorned the streets and temples of the capital. In republican times devotion to art was discouraged and despised. Marcellus, who captured
Syracuse, was severely blamed for introducing the
taste for Greek art into Rome, and thus diverting
the attention of the citizens from more useful
pursuits. Cicero in the trial of Verres explains to
the jury that the Greeks attach a quite unaccount-
able importance to the works of certain sculptors,
of which Verres had deprived them. Even in our
period, when the fire under Nero destroyed an
innumerable quantity of precious masterpieces, his-

torians content themselves with mentioning the
bare fact, without regret or comment. There was,
however, growing up a sentiment of admiration for
art, which never, indeed, developed into an intelli-
gent appreciation, but shewed itself in a widespread dilettantism and passion for collecting, and
a great deal of pretence of knowledge. It was
common for these amateurs to profess that they
were able to distinguish the works of one great
master from another, and to discover at a glance
a spurious imitation. Antique bronzes could be
tested, so they averred, by the smell. Trimalchio
tells his guests that he would give up anything
rather than his faculty as an art critic—a talent
which he proceeds to illustrate by the most absurd
blunders in explaining the mythological subjects in
his collection. It was, indeed, inevitable that the
Romans, in patronising an art which they did not
understand and seldom tried to practise, should
appear in the light of *parvenus* who fill their
houses with masterpieces which they cannot appreciate, or with imitations which they cannot detect.
The chief exceptions to this insensibility seem to
be Pliny the Younger and Lucian, especially the
latter. Pliny took a genuine pleasure in the Corin-

thian statuettes and other works of art with which
he adorned his houses ; and Lucian, when he mentions the subject, shows a fine discrimination, more
Greek than Roman. The causes of this defect in
Roman cultivation seem to be three. First, the
natural incapacity of the Roman mind to understand and appreciate artistic genius : next, the low
position occupied by most sculptors and painters,
who were generally either slaves or freedmen :
and, thirdly, the want of life and originality in the
artistic world itself, which prevented it from exciting public interest or claiming public admiration.
This last reason may be, perhaps, demurred to.
We do not find it easy to associate the notion of
decline with the age which produced, *e.g.*, the
Laocoon group*, or the majestic portrait-statue of
Nerva. But we have now unfortunately lost most
of the splendid Greek originals which gave a model
to all sculptors of the Roman age—works of genius
which completely threw into the shade the feebler
efforts of ἡ δουλὴ Ἑλλάς. The most skilful imitations (and some of them are works of great talent)
could not arouse the same enthusiasm as new crea-
tions from the hand of a real genius ; and the con-

---

* The latest authorities on archæology now ascribe this statue
to an earlier date.

sciousness of this deterioration may have had much to do with the flagging interest which the public took in the painter's or sculptor's studio.

Virgil was right in naming sculpture as the art in which " others " most excelled his countrymen. Very few men of Italian birth attempted sculpture. It was then and for ever the birthright of the Greeks, and no Roman attempted to dispute that supremacy. The modern writer is tempted to linger with mixed wonder and regret over this most exquisite product of the old civilisation. When we visit London, and come suddenly upon one of the grotesque statues with which our metropolis is disfigured, we cannot help marvelling how an art once so perfect should have been so completely lost. What must have been the beauty of a city of the ancient world, where every street, every temple, every open space, was ennobled by those exquisite forms of marble and bronze, the mutilated remnants of which are the greatest feast for modern eyes ? These triumphs of human genius, which had formerly been the pride of every Greek city, from Massilia to Asia Minor, were now for the most part transferred to Rome and other Italian towns. The discovery of

Herculaneum and Pompeii first revealed to us
how widely diffused was the possession of statuary,
and how rich even second-class towns were in
this species of embellishment. As to Rome
itself, it was crowded with statues. Every open
space in the city was occupied by monumental
figures of eminent citizens, and the Thermæ,
temples, and other public buildings were decorated
by the spoils of many a Greek city. These statues
may be divided into three classes—those which
were dedicated to religion, those which were
erected as monuments to particular persons, and
those which were merely ornamental. With
regard to the first, the numerous temples were
adorned with a large number of statues representing deities, which were very often votive
offerings; and family worship also had its
images, generally of a humbler kind. Nero,
for example, like Louis XIV., was superstitiously
devoted to certain images, and carried about
with him an "icuncula puellaris" as a charm.
Such images were much used by travellers to
protect them against shipwreck. The second
class of statues, those which were put up as monuments, were still more numerous and important.

The custom of erecting statues to distinguished men had existed at Rome for a long time, as well as that of filling the atrium with wax masks representing ancestors. But the Empire developed the usage to an extent unheard of before. The statues and busts of the emperors alone were visible in every street, and almost every house. They were protected by the most tyrannical legislation, so that to mutilate or destroy one of them was a crime punished by death, and even to strip or beat a slave in sight of a bust of the emperor might be made a capital offence. Hence, slaves were accustomed to fly for refuge to these statues, and the tyranny of the Cæsars may indirectly have saved many slaves from the fury of their masters. Not only was it treason to shew disrespect to the image of the reigning emperor, but those of his predecessors who had obtained divine honours were protected with the same severity. A few of the worst tyrants, however, received different treatment. The statues and busts of Nero and Domitian were broken and hurled down by the exulting populace immediately after their deaths, so that very few representations of them remained. The same posthumous vengeance was shewn to the statues of Sejanus, who had filled Rome with portrait-images of himself. In a few hours after the death of the detested minister, the face, which had lately been the second in the whole world, was made into " pitchers and pans and kettles and pots."* A more economical but less usual plan was to decapitate the statues of the deceased emperor, and place the head of his successor on the shoulders. This, however, was deemed disrespectful, and was only resorted to in rare instances, *e.g.*, the Colossus of Nero, which bore several heads before Commodus transformed it into a Hercules, after his own likeness. Statues of private persons, both living and dead, were extremely numerous. In republican days this had been a distinction ; now every one might have a statue, and if he had no friends or clients to give him one he might put it up himself. Even circus jockeys had their statues, with their horses and chariots. The Forum became so full that on one occasion at least it had to be cleared. Absurd as this custom was, it must have added very much to the beauty of a town, provided that the statues were good, as they generally were.

* Juv. 10. 56, &c.

Statues of a purely ornamental or artistic kind were also very numerous. It was this kind of sculpture which was taken in such quantities from the Greek cities. Some of the emperors, especially Nero, plundered the eastern provinces of their works of art to a shameful extent, the statues being used partly in the decoration of the palace and partly in that of baths, theatres, &c. Private persons were equally assiduous in collecting, and no wealthy family was without its gallery of sculpture. Of the character of the decorative statues we can judge from those which have been discovered; some, perhaps the largest number, represented gods or mythological scenes, thus combining religion with art, as in modern times; others were studies of some favourite subject, such as a boy wrestling with a goose, or an athlete preparing for a contest; the majority were copies or imitations of some Greek original. The wide diffusion of this branch of art is quite unparallelled in later times; it gave all classes of the community the advantages which are now confined to a few, and enabled the citizen to have images of grace and beauty constantly before his eyes.

The art of painting was less exclusively con-

H

fined to the Greeks than that of sculpture. From Fabius Pictor, the historian, downwards, several Romans painted, and lessons in drawing and painting were given in high-class schools. Unfortunately very little of ancient pictorial art has been preserved to us. We have enough to make us deeply regret that we have no more, but not enough to give us a clear idea of the characteristic features of classical painting. We know, however, that it was as widely diffused as the sister art, and that Rome was full of pictures, both decorative and monumental. Just as statues were erected to commemorate persons and events, so pictures were publicly exhibited for the same purpose. In triumphs and public celebrations pictures always formed part of the show. It is characteristic of the Romans that pictorial representations were often made to take the place of placards, advertisements, and votive tablets. Even in the law court one of the parties would sometimes present the jury with a series of pictures to illustrate the disreputable habits of his opponent. Beggars carried large boards painted with the history of their misfortunes—the fire or the shipwreck which had deprived them of their worldly goods. The

temples of the gods were full of votive pictures, so
that Isis, who saved men from shipwreck, was the
best patroness of painters. Private houses were
always decorated with graceful wall-paintings representing scenes, figures, fruit and flowers, or
mere patterns. For the most part Roman wall-
decoration seems to have been far superior to ours,
and to have frequently reached a high degree of
artistic beauty. Many admirable pictures were
painted on house-walls, or worked in mosaic on
the floor. Another use of painting was in the
illustration of books, which often contained a
portrait of the author or a representation of his
subject on the title-page. Portrait painting was
very common, but we have no means of knowing
whether it was well done or not. It appears that
painters often gratified the vanity of their sitters
by improving their features in the portrait. We
see then that painting, both decorative and otherwise, was as universal in the first century as it is
now. The extent of the art is the more remarkable, when we remember that the Romans had
none of those mechanical aids—printing of wall-
papers, engraving, photography, &c.—which have
so largely increased the number of artistic designs

in every place in Europe. It is improbable that
the early empire *surpassed* modern Europe in the
diffusion of painting, since these aids to multiplication have been discovered; but the vast quantity
which evidently existed speaks highly for the
artistic energy of the old civilisation.

Of the third of the fine arts, music, we do not
propose to say much. Although our music is, to a
great extent, derived, by continuous tradition, from
that of the ancients, there is a wide difference
between them. Music, among the Greeks and
Romans, was far simpler and plainer, and, so to
speak, less ambitious. A piece of lyric poetry set
to music, as all lyric poetry was meant to be, was
not disguised, but elucidated by the tune. The
air merely brought out the sense, and was sub-
servient to it : the words were the first thing, the
music the second. In longer pieces, such as Ovid's
Elegiacs, which were sung and danced to at the
theatres, the music must have been a mere re-
citative. We have, of course, no examples of
ancient music to judge by, but to all appearance
the Italians were then, as now, noted for their fine
ear and critical appreciation of music. The chief
instruments used were the lyre and the flute, each

of which was modified in several different forms. The chief places where music was performed were the theatres, where it was an indispensable part of the entertainment, and private houses, where trained choirs of slaves were employed to sing and play to the guests at dinner, or for the delectation of their master alone. In our century complaints, no doubt well founded, were made that the art of music was being corrupted by popular innovations in style, and still more by the sensual character of the new compositions, which pandered to the worst tastes of the populace. Singers and players from Spain and from the eastern provinces did much to spread this evil. But the most characteristic feature of our period is not the degradation of music, but the abatement of the national prejudice against it. In republican days a Roman would have been ashamed to own himself a skilled musician, and a matron would have considered such an accomplishment highly derogatory to her dignity. Now both sexes gave themselves to a study of music with an eagerness which did not, indeed, pass unrebuked, but was not in any way checked by the upholders of ancient prejudices. Great, indeed, was the change from the time when

Scipio Æmilianus delivered a scathing invective in
the senate against schools of music and dancing,
at one of which he had even seen the son of a
Roman magistrate! Now music, at least, was part
of a liberal education, and probably most boys of
good position attended lessons in singing and harp-
playing. Nero was, of course, the greatest patron
of the art. He, in fact, was so completely eman-
cipated from the traditions and prejudices of his
countrymen, that he loved best to pose as a professional artist, and exhibited his skill in public,
like any Greek *citharœdus.* This, it is true, gave
the greatest offence, but the enthusiasm of the
emperor for music gave a stimulus to the practice
of the art, among other ways by leading to the
foundation of a musical contest held at Rome.
Women of good family also studied music, and
even composed their own melodies. So far had
the old order changed under the influence of Greek
manners and new luxury !

CHAPTER VI.

GRADES OF SOCIETY.

WE propose in this chapter to give a sketch of the component parts of Roman society, from the palace to the hovel. The gradations of rank were always rather strongly marked at Rome, and the taste for external decorations was kept up under the Empire as much as under the Republic. Hence, in spite of the democratic basis of the Empire, there were still lines of demarcation between the senator and the knight, and between the citizen and the provincial, as well as the broad difference between the free-born and the slave. Between the magistrate at Rome and his porter were many intermediate grades, sharply defined in theory, though often overstepped in practice. It will be well to take these in order, noticing on the way whatever seems interesting or characteristic in the various occupations of the community.

The Cæsars had, properly speaking, no court.

Their households resembled those of ordinary Roman nobles. Such system of etiquette as there was was only designed to keep out intruders from the palace, not to make the monarchy more imposing. Hence there were none of those court officials who now surround every palace—men of noble birth who feel honoured by holding some post in the royal household. No Cæsar employed senators or their wives to perform menial offices for him : such attendants as he required were chosen from the class of slaves or freedmen. Even honourable and responsible posts, such as that of secretary, were filled by freedmen. This was exclusively the case under the earlier emperors, but Tacitus* says that Vitellius in his short reign introduced the innovation of employing knights for these posts instead of freedmen. Vespasian and Titus may have followed his example, but Domitian appears to have reverted to the old plan, and Spartianus† says that Hadrian was the first to employ a knight as secretary. We must, then, remember that the permanent posts about the palace were held by men of low extraction, who had generally once been slaves. These freedmen had generally

* Tac. H. 1. 58.   † Spartian. Hadr. 58.

gained their advancement by their own qualities. Under good emperors they were often able and trustworthy men ; under the worst, they were often the vilest of their sex. In either case a precarious but very great power was in their hands, and they often amassed fortunes unheard of before, and hardly equalled anywhere until the present century. Pallas had three hundred millions of sesterces, Narcissus four hundred millions ; and others became nearly as rich. The chief offices at court which we hear of are the control of the accounts (*a rationibus*), that of petitions (*a libellis*), and the post of private secretary (*ab epistulis*). [Important administrative offices were usually given to men of higher rank, particularly to the knights. The freedmen who attained high posts were generally Greeks, rarely Syrians, Egyptians, or Gauls.]

The court ceremonial was, as we have said, very slight. It chiefly consisted in the morning visit of the emperor's friends, a custom which was by no means confined to the court, but was practised habitually by the friends and clients of wealthy nobles. The only difference was that owing to the crowds of persons who wished to pay their respects to the emperor it was necessary to have guards round the gates, and to search visitors who might be suspected of meditating treason. Even these precautions were not always adopted. Generally speaking those only might call in this way who were included in the list of the emperor's "friends," a term which came to have a very definite signification. The "friends" of the emperor were divided into three classes, of which the first consisted of senators and other magnates, the second chiefly of knights and others of a less exalted station than the first class, while the third contained persons who had won favour with the emperor by their own gifts— poets, rhetoricians, philosophers, and such like. Sometimes a token was given to these privileged persons, by which they might gain admittance. This institution of "friends" was also a development of a republican custom. Both in these morning visits, and when dining with the emperor, the toga was always worn.

Leaving the palace, we come next to the Senate, that once august assembly which might boast the proudest traditions of any aristocratic body in the world. The old families, whose names appeared so often in the consular Fasti, had most of them died out before the end of our period. Civil war, proscriptions, and celibacy, had made sad havoc of their ranks before the beginning of the century, and the decay went on even in the peaceful reigns which followed. Their places were filled by new men of various classes. Some were knights of good parentage, promoted according to custom to the superior rank; others were obscure citizens whom fortune or merit had advanced; others were Italians and even provincials. Julius Cæsar bore the reproach of being the first to introduce trousered Gauls into the Senate, but his example was followed by his successors, and the "right of senatorship" became a coveted privilege in provincial towns. Even sons of freedmen had become senators before the reign of Nero, who tried in vain to stop the abuse. Before the end of the century many senatorial families were of servile descent. The means by which these parvenus made their way into the senate were, of course, very various. Military reputation was, perhaps, the rarest and most honourable. Personal services to the emperor, among which the most common was the infamous trade of informer, were an easier and more usual road to rank and dignity. The influx of these new men did not at all diminish the respect with which society regarded such of the old families as still survived. Indeed, the tendency was to pay an exaggerated deference to noble birth, and to excuse in an Æmilius or Silanus faults which would have been fatal to the reputation of an ordinary man. Juvenal in one of his best known satires, bears testimony to the absurd respect paid to old families, whose halls were full of the battered and blackened effigies of republican heroes, and adorned with pedigrees reaching even to Olympus. His vigorous assertions " miserum est aliorum incumbere famæ," "nobilitas sola est atque unica virtus," only shew how far the contrary opinion prevailed in the vulgar mind. Additional testimony to the interest taken in genealogies is furnished by the records of books on the subject. Varro wrote a treatise on those families which claimed Trojan descent. Atticus had explored the antiquities of noble families. Messala, under Augustus, wrote on the same subject. Nor did the taste wane in the next generation. We hear of fictitious genealogies being manufactured for *nouveaux riches* ; and Vespasian on his accession found flatterers anxious to make him a pedigree. Senators of old family, who had become so empoverished as no longer to possess the " senatorial census" of 1,200,000 sesterces, were often subsidized from the Imperial exchequer to save them from losing their rank. The sons of men of " senatorial family" became senators as matter of of course, and the old custom of allowing them as children to attend the debates with their fathers was revived. By degrees the Senate became a kind of hereditary peerage, instead of the selected body of former days.* The dignity of the senator was kept up by several external privileges. He was distinguished by the broad purple border of his toga, and by his black sandals adorned by a silver crescent; special seats were reserved for his order at the public games, and he might dine in the Capitol at the public expense. But much of his consideration doubtless rested on the wealth which he usually possessed. The limit of 1,200,000 sesterces was intended to exclude poor men from the order, but in most cases senators

---

* This change was, of course, not consummated till long after the first century.

possessed many times that modest sum. Many
of them were owners of immense estates or mines
in the provinces. In Nero's reign half the province of Africa belonged to six great landlords.
On the other hand, they were forbidden to increase
their capital by trade or commerce of any kind,
so that it was not easy for them to recover from
any pecuniary loss. This gave some excuse for
the assistance given them in such cases by the
emperor, which was sometimes supplemented by
the generosity of their own order. The calls
upon their purse were also very heavy. House-
rent in the fashionable quarters of Rome was very
high, and a considerable amount of state had to
be kept up, including generally an army of clients
and poor dependants, who stuck like leeches to
their rich patron. Public life was also very
burdensome with its shows and games and other
expenses for the benefit of the people ; so that we
are not surprised to find that senatorial families
were often in difficulties.

Before going on to the knights, the second order
in the state, we should mention the high honours
paid to the consuls and other great magistrates.
Although shorn of all real power, these republican

dignities were as much prized as when Rome was
a free state. Even the custom of appointing
several consuls in one year did not materially
lessen the estimation in which the honour was
held. The magistrate during his year of office
was looked up to and revered as much as if he
were still the holder of real authority, and on his
part he was expected to do nothing which could
compromise the dignity of his office. We are surprised at the energy with which Juvenal declaims
against the consul who drove his chariot himself
"in the night indeed, but under the accusing eyes
of the stars." The higher priesthoods were regarded with as much ambition as the civil magistracies, with which they were often conjoined.

The knights were less successful in preserving
the dignity of their order than the senators. On
account of their numbers, which were not limited
like that of the senate, it was not difficult for
persons to assume the insignia of a knight without proper title, and the emperors helped towards
the degradation of the order by allowing even
slaves on manumission to wear the gold ring.*

* See an interesting collection of passages bearing on this subject in Mayor's Juvenal, note on Satire 7. 16.

In fact the ordo equester was becoming merged in
the main body of citizens, though the fusion did
not take place till after our period. Except at Rome,
the knights were of course the highest rank, and
the law which limited the dignity to persons possessed of more than 400,000 sesterces seems to
have been generally observed. Many families,
both at Rome and in the principal towns, were
hereditary knights, and these were accustomed to
look down upon those who had obtained the dignity by military adventure or the gift of fortune.
The knights still monopolised the lucrative financial
posts which had belonged to them under the
Republic, and many of them exercised those commercial professions from which the senators were
by law debarred. Hence some knights preferred
to remain in the second order when they might·
have entered the senate, and this choice, which was
dictated sometimes by economy, and sometimes
by love of ease and want of ambition, was praised
as moderation. Mæcenas is the best known instance
of a distinguished man who refused senatorial rank,
but he appears to have had many imitators. These
knights with senatorial census were formed into a
distinct class, and were called *equites insignes, splen-*

didi, or *illustres.* It does not appear that all knights
with the higher census were *equites illustres,* but
only those on whom the honour was conferred
by the emperor. They were even to be allowed to
wear the *latus clavus* like senators. This tended
still further to lower the main body of the knights,
who possessed only the property qualification.

We now come to the professional class in the
Roman community. The doctors, schoolmasters,
lecturers, and professors of the capital were generally Greeks, who, in fact, monopolised to a great
extent all the learned professions with the exception of the bar. Some of these Greeks were of
servile extraction ; others had come over to Rome
for the sake of profit and fame. Some were even
actually slaves, whose fees and payments belonged
de jure to their master, though they were often
allowed to retain part of them as *peculium.* This,
to some extent, lowered the estimation of the
learned professions, and deterred citizens of good
family from entering them—one of the unhappy
consequences of slavery. The bar was, as we
have said, the chief exception. The profession of
advocate was one of the chief roads to success
open to the aspiring young Roman. His educa-

tion had been largely directed to the art of rhetoric, and the fame of the orator was the most common object of ambition in his class. As a rule he did not trouble himself much with the intricacies of the law, but gave his whole attention to public speaking. It often happened that an advocate had no special knowledge of the legal question at issue, but trusted entirely to his eloquence to win him his case. We shall be less surprised at this when we remember the great latitude allowed to pleaders in ancient times, and the prominence in all the extant speeches of invective and declamation as compared with legal argument and evidence. It was customary, however, for the orator to retain the services of a *pragmaticus,* a lawyer of lower grade in estimation, who was prepared to give advice on legal questions.

The best days of Roman oratory were passed when Augustus made himself master of the Empire. Rome never produced a second Cicero, or even a second Hortensius. This falling off was partly due to the loss of liberty that attended the end of the republic, but partly, also, to the increased difficulty with which a poor and unknown man could make his way to the front. Juvenal*

* Satire 7.

declares indignantly that in his day even Cicero
would not earn two pounds at the bar unless he
wore a large and conspicuous gold ring. The man
who wishes to succeed, he says, must be seen in
the streets, borne in a litter by a number of young
Medes, making purchases of plate and "murra"
vases and beautiful slaves; he must wear a
brilliant robe of purple, and live in a splendid
house with an equestrian statue of himself in the
vestibule. Such a man may demand the highest
price allowed by law for his pleading; but
eloquence is rarely found, he says, with a thread-
bare coat. While an Æmilius, with his noble
name and his wealth, can ask 10,000 sesterces for
a single pleading, the poor and obscure orator can
only get one *aureus* for four, and even that is reduced by the attorney's fees. A jockey at the
circus could make more than a hundred pleaders.
We can hardly be surprised if some of these ill-paid
barristers were led to take up questionable cases
and to endeavour to make a name by quackery.
It does not appear that the first ever caused much
scruple to a Roman lawyer, nor should we condemn, in the circumstances, the deception of
wearing a hired ring to give the appearance of

wealth, nor the custom of employing *claqueurs* to applaud the good points of a speech. If success as a pleader was once achieved the orator's prospects were very brilliant. Some of the most prominent " new men," both in our century and in that which preceded it, owed their elevation to this cause. The name of the famous advocate was on everyone's lips; his house was besieged by friends and clients, and he might make a large fortune by his practice.*

In fact the legal profession was generally looked upon as a lucrative one. Martial is advised by a friend to plead instead of writing poetry, in order to make his fortune.† The poet gives the same advice to Valerius Flaccus.‡ These statements are not at all incompatible with the lugubrious account of Juvenal. The successful pleaders were few, the " briefless barristers" were many. For these last it might be the best chance to follow the poet's advice, and leaving the ungrateful capital to seek an opening in Gaul or Africa, or even among

---

* Some interesting facts on this head are given by Tacitus. Dial. de Orat.

† Mart. 1. 17, " Et dicit mihi sæpe, Magna res est." See also 2. 30, " Dives eris, si causas egeris, inquit."

‡ Mart. 1. 76. 13, " Illic " (in the Forum) " æra sonant : " &c.

the Britons, who were learning eloquence from the ready-tongued Gauls.* The other alternative was to stay at home and eke out the profits of pleading by giving lectures. Those who were less successful as pleaders sometimes made a reputation as teachers of rhetoric, and we hear of distinguished advocates giving instruction in oratory after ceasing to practise. We shall probably come to the conclusion that except for the greater importance attached at Rome to the study of eloquence, the conditions of the legal profession bore a close resemblance to the state of things at the present day.

If we turn to the profession of teaching, we shall find that it ranked rather lower at Rome than in most civilised societies. It was the same at Athens. Demosthenes, when he is drawing contrasts to his own advantage between Æschines and himself, makes it his climax, " *You* were teaching grammar, while *I* was a schoolboy." "What an unworthy thing to do !" exclaims Annius Florus, " how patiently you endure sitting in school and teaching boys !" The causes of this disparagement of the profession were probably the

* Juv. 15. 112 ; 7. 148.

servile associations of the *pædagogi*, the small pay,
and the generally small acquirements of the
schoolmasters at Rome. The social position of
the schoolmaster began to improve at the end of
the republic. Plotius was the first Roman teacher
of rhetoric, in Cicero's boyhood.* Seneca mentions Blandus, a Roman knight, as the teacher of
Fabianus, adding, however, that "before him this
most noble profession had been left to freedmen,
and there was a strange idea that it was disgraceful
to teach what it was honourable to learn." By
the time of Juvenal it had become one of the recognised careers for a Roman of the middle class.
With regard to the profits of the profession, it was
a subject of complaint in Ovid's time—

> "Nec vos turba deam censu fraudata magistri
>   Spernite."

and matters do not seem to have improved much
for teachers in the first century, A.D. Juvenal
says that the yearly fee (not "*income*" surely, as
Mayor ad loc.) of a grammarian was only that
which a jockey received for a single race. This
was one "aureus," a sum which is very small of

---

* Gellius (15. 11) quotes a most characteristic censorial edict
against Latin "rhetors," published in 92 B.C.

course, but which would mean a competence if the class was large. The picture which he draws of the life of a teacher is certainly unpleasant enough. Besides the monotony of teaching the same things again and again, and the anxiety of the moral supervision of a number of boys, it appears that parents often tried to evade payment of the fee on pretence that the boy had learned nothing.

> " Rara tamen merces quæ cognitione tribuni
>   Non egeat."
> " Mercedem appellas?   Quid enim scio ?" &c.

The grammarian was also liable to be pestered by questions intended to test his knowledge. He could not walk to the baths without meeting parents and others who accosted him with such questions as " Who was Hecuba's mother?" "What was the name of the nurse of Anchises ?" "What was the tune that the Sirens used to sing?" Ignorance of these important facts might lose him a pupil or give the parent an excuse for withholding his fee. He had also, it appears, to put up with insults from his class, who gave him nicknames, and even struck him.* It was the custom to begin work very early in the morning, even before it was light, so that idle citizens were disturbed in their repose

* Juv. 7. 217.

by the sounds of the class—the "verba et verbera"
with which knowledge was driven into the head
of the "Arcadian youth."* But these trials were
not always without their compensations. In particular, the teacher of rhetoric, who ranked generally higher than the mere grammarian, sometimes
made a good income from his profession. Good
fortune, like that of Verrius Flaccus, who was employed by Augustus to teach his grandchildren at
a salary of 26,000 sesterces, was, of course, rare ;
but we have instances of masters who made a
much larger income. Quintilian, for example, had
several parks† ; Remmius Palæmon drew from his
school no less than 400,000 sesterces a year,‡ and
other instances of successful teachers might be
quoted.§ On the whole, however, the profession
of teaching was a good deal less remunerative than
that of the law.

Of the literary profession, which shares with the
law and the school the Seventh Satire of Juvenal,
we do not intend to say much here. The restric-

* Juv. 7. 225. 160.   Mart. 9. 30. 12. 57. 9. 68.
† Juv. 7. 189.
‡ Suet. Gr. Ill. 23.
§ Teachers of arithmetic and book-keeping generally had larger
classes than grammarians.   Mart. 10. 62. 4 ; Hor. A. P. 325, &c.

tions and dangers which surrounded the poet and historian belong to the subject of politics; the character of their productions will be more fitly treated under the head of culture. Juvenal of course treats the matter from the pecuniary point of view, which is the subject of his satire. He complains of the want of patronage extended to authors by the rich and great, and contrasts the unhappy condition of the poet in his time with the honours and wealth lavished upon Virgil. There was probably some reason in the complaint, though the greatest authors have generally shewn themselves indifferent about profit. Martial speaks quite in the same strain of the stinginess of his patrons. This hunting for gifts and pensions sounds rather sordid to us; but we must remember that a writer could hardly earn a competence by the mere sale of his books. The relations between author and publisher at Rome are somewhat obscure, but it does not appear that the author often got a good bargain. In fact we do not know of any case in which payment for copyright is mentioned. Pliny was surprised to hear that copies of his works were being sold at Lugdunum.* Martial, on

* Ep. 9. 11.

the other hand, urges a stingy friend to buy, rather than to borrow, his Epigrams.*　The price of books was so small that neither author nor publisher could have made much profit.　We hear of a volume of Martial being offered for about four-pence, while a handsomely bound copy could be had for five denarii.†

In most cases the author did not attempt to make a profit by selling copies of his works, but looked to his patrons and friends, and especially to the emperor, for remuneration.　This unsatisfactory arrangement is responsible for much of the syco-phancy and adulation which disgraces Roman literature.　In our period, even this expedient was seldom successful, and the author who had only his pen to depend upon was usually in great poverty.　It is very noteworthy that no one was too proud to accept direct pecuniary assistance.　Pliny not only sent Martial "viaticum" for his last journey to Spain, but gave a present of between three and four hundred pounds to Quintilian, who was not at all a poor man.　In spite, however, of the smallness of the profit, authors were naturally proud of their profession, and not inclined to ex-

* Mart. 1. 117.　　　　　　† Mart. 1. 118.

change it for the more lucrative occupations of the advocate or the vine grower.*

The army sometimes opened a career for young men of good family. The knights in particular often entered a profession where their rank ensured them favour and promotion.† They were appointed to the command of a cohort, or even of a legion, without much merit or exertion on their part.‡ Men of the third order seldom rose higher than the post of centurion or military tribune. The army had, however, other attractions besides the chances of high promotion. It still enjoyed a good deal of social consideration, and the immense power which it now possessed collectively gave a good deal of prestige and influence to its individual members. The immunity enjoyed by the soldier for deeds of violence is a frequent subject of complaint. Soldiers frequently insulted, assaulted, and robbed peaceable citizens with impunity. " It is easier," says a contemporary writer, " to get a false verdict against a civilian than a true one against a soldier." The officers, too, might obtain lucrative posts. Besides the most dignified, and probably

* Mart. 1. 17. † Juv. 1. 58, " Cui fas curam sperare cohortis."
‡ Cf. Hor., " Quod mihi pareret legio Romana tribuno." This, however, was more characteristic of the civil wars than of the Empire.

richest offices, such as Prefect of public safety,
Superintendent of the corn distribution, Governor
of Egypt, and Prefect of the Prætorian camp,
there were minor financial posts which it was
now customary to give to officers. These prizes
of the profession were, of course, almost monopolised by the knights.

Farming was rather an occupation than a profession for the better class. In spite of the old
honourable traditions of the citizen-farmer, agri-
culture did not hold out sufficient inducements
either socially or pecuniarily to tempt many to
give up the amusements and society of the capital.
It is true that Martial, in one place, says " Res
magna est Tite, quam facit colonus," but elsewhere
he laughs at farmers who have to buy even their
garden produce at Rome."*

The profession of medicine, though often very
lucrative, did not rank so high socially as in
modern times. Its practice was almost confined

* We do not forget the maxim of Cato, that the most lucrative
profession is "bene pascere;" the next, "to be a tolerable grazier;" and the third, "to be a mediocre grazier:" but in our
period sheep-farms were managed without the personal superintendence of their owner, and thus could not be said to make
him a profession. Cato's remark is also directed against corn-
farming.

to foreigners,* and was to a large extent in the hands of freedmen, and even of slaves. The oriental provinces of the empire supplied the greatest number of physicians and surgeons. Most of the celebrated practitioners whose names have come down to us have Greek names; but we hear Egyptians and Syrians spoken of as skilful doctors, and not a few, such as Antonius Musa under Augustus, and Vettius Valens under Claudius, were either freedmen with Italian names or actually Romans of pure blood. The old practice had been for wealthy families to keep slaves skilled in the medical art, who prescribed for themselves and their households, and brought additional profit to their owners by practising for pay in other houses. In the time of the empire, though many able physicians and surgeons belonged to this class, the majority had a more independent position. We hear frequently of "family doctors," who were paid a fixed sum annually for their attendance and advice, and of distinguished physicians who combined teaching with their practice, and paid their visits attended

* Cf. Plin. N. H. 29. 11, "Solam hanc Græcarum artium nondum exercet Romana gravitas."

by a troop of students. These successful doctors
often made large fortunes, larger probably than
even a brilliant advocate. The elder Pliny* mentions by name five who in his day made 250,000
sesterces (about £2,000) a year. He also tells
us that† Stertinius made a favour of accepting the
post of court physician to Claudius at a salary of
500,000 sesterces, since he might have made
600,000 by private practice. This distinguished
practitioner and his brother left behind them
conjointly the sum of 30 millions of sesterces,
though they had made large donations in
their lifetime to the city of Naples. A little
further on he tells us of another, Crinas of Mar-
seilles, who after an open-handed life left ten
millions, while a less fortunate surgeon was
mulcted in that sum by the Emperor Claudius.
A few instances of exorbitant fees have come
down to us. Pliny mentions 200,000 sesterces
being paid by an ex-prætor afflicted with leprosy;
but he does not say how long the treatment was
continued. There is no direct evidence as to the
ordinary amount of a doctor's fee. It does not
appear that any precautions were taken by law to

* Plin. H. N. 29. 5.   † Id. 8, 9.

prevent incompetent and disreputable persons
from offering their services as physicians or
surgeons. The profession was often entered
without any further qualification than an agreeable manner and a supply of effrontery. Men
left other professions to take up medicine without
any special preparation for the science, and succeeded or failed according to the popular verdict
on their powers. It is not to be wondered at,
that in these circumstances a great deal of
quackery and not a little crime was found in
the ranks of the profession. Doctors were frequently accused of gross incompetence, of improper familiarity with their female patients, and
even of poisoning for their own sakes or for
money. The famous Hippocratic oath, which so
nobly sets forth the duty of a high-minded votary
of Æsculapius, was hardly in accordance with
the practice of the majority of Roman doctors.
Pliny complains that surgeons try experiments on
their patients, and that a doctor is the only man
who may kill people with impunity.

It may be doubted whether medical science
advanced much in this period. Ancient surgeons
seem always to have been prone to the use of

the knife and cautery. Archagathus, one of the first Greek physicians who came to Rome, was especially notorious for his cruelty. Some of the prescriptions which have come down to us sound as absurd as those of the middle ages. Modern physicians would probably shake their heads at the cold water cure of Antonius Musa, which is said to have saved Augustus' life, and probably destroyed that of Marcellus : a mixture of salt and vinegar is ordered for quinsy, and gout is treated with an application of goat's feet to the chest, and a diet of frogs cooked in oil. Specialism, however, was carried to a great extent. We hear of doctors for both sexes, of dentists, oculists, ear-doctors, &c. Various schools of medicine are also mentioned, among which we may mention the " Wine-givers," who were doubtless popular. A copious draught of wine, followed by a bath, was a favourite prescription of this school.

The law, the army, education, literature, more rarely farming and medicine, were the chief occupations which Roman society regarded as worthy of a gentleman. Descending a step lower in the social scale, we come to trades of various kinds, one of the most lucrative of which was that of the *præco* or crier and auctioneer, a fact which seems to indicate that property changed hands very rapidly at Rome. Another prominent trade was that of the *fullers*, who whitened and mended dirty and torn togas. The *purple* trade is also characteristic. The *barbers'* shops were much frequented for the sake of gossip; and barbers often made large fortunes. Juvenal speaks of a *tonsor* owning an innumerable number of villas, and Martial of another whom his mistress had raised to the rank of *eques* by a large present of money. Architects, sculptors, and painters generally belonged to the tradesman class. So did the important maritime merchants, who carried on the foreign trade of Italy, and conveyed luxuries to Rome from every quarter of the known world.

Trades-guilds, not unlike those of the middle ages, existed at Rome from the very earliest period, their origin being ascribed to Numa. They were nine in number originally, but others were added later. They each had a meeting-house of their own, and rules of their society, and religious ceremonies which were performed at public gatherings of the guild.

K

Another important trade was that of the *caupones*, or inn-keepers, who seem to have been generally Orientals, often Syrians. The keeper of a *popina* was despised, and his trade regarded as disreputable, not only on account of the dishonesty of which he was accused, but because the inns and eating-houses were often used for debauchery and vicious purposes. Drunkenness seems to have been common at some of these low haunts, which were frequented not merely by slaves and vagabonds, but by dissipated members of the upper classes.

The last trade we shall mention here is that of bookselling. This was a very flourishing business, as large libraries were frequent at Rome, both public ones—of which there were at last no less than twenty-eight—and private collections, several of which contained upwards of twenty or thirty thousand volumes. The multiplication of copies was effected entirely by slaves, who copied so fast and cheaply that the cost of books was even less than at the present day.*

* Sir G. Lewis (Credibility of Roman History, 1. 197) says, "It may be doubted whether there were ever a hundred copies of Virgil or Horace in existence at any time before the invention of printing." I believe this statement to be entirely erroneous.

The unfortunate contempt for trade, which had been bred at Rome by warlike habits, had survived the state of things which produced it. The Roman citizen was still debarred by an unreasonable pride from those humble pursuits which in healthy communities give occupation to and provide a maintenance for the majority of the population. There was in consequence a large number of persons who had no regular means of livelihood, and who were obliged to depend on others for their support. The poorest class, very numerous in the capital, was provided with a daily dole of bread by the state. That above them, comprising a large part of the third order or middle class, was to a great extent dependent on that peculiar Roman institution, the *clientela*. Like almost everything else, it was not an invention of the empire, but a modification of an old custom. Under the republic the clients rendered real services to their patrons, and the relations between them were not unlike those between lord and vassal in the healthier time of feudalism. In such relations there was no loss of dignity on either side. The

Among other evidence for the abundance of books, we may notice that Augustus confiscated 2,000 copies of the pseudo-Sibylline books in Rome alone.

K 2

patron gave his client his powerful protection and assistance in case of need, and the client repaid the obligation by faithful and honourable service to the patron. Under the empire this institution had ceased to have any real value. The patron no longer needed the adherence of his client except for purposes of ostentation, and the client stood in small need of protection from his patron, except in the form of pecuniary assistance. Hence the relations between patron and client became degraded on both sides. On the one side pride and insolence, on the other servility and avarice, became the characteristics of the two parties. The duties of the client were, in the first place, to call upon his patron early in the morning, a sufficiently troublesome obligation considering the unpleasant and even dangerous condition of the streets, and the necessity of wearing the uncomfortable toga. Then he had to hold himself constantly in readiness to accompany his patron on a walk or journey, and to perform any little services that he might require. Lastly, he had to observe a strict and even humiliating deference, never omitting to address his patron by the word " Domine," and paying him every kind of flattery and attention. As a recompense for these irksome duties, the client received a small payment in money, called *sportula*, the origin of which is a matter of dispute, but it was probably at first an allowance of food instead of a meal at the patron's house. The client might also expect occasional invitations to dine with his patron—a doubtful boon, since it was not uncommon for the host to remind his guest of his inferior position by humiliating treatment, providing him with inferior food and wine, and allowing his domestics to neglect and insult him. This behaviour was doubtless confined to the vulgar *nouveaux riches*, but we can hardly be surprised at small consideration being shewn to a class of men who willingly placed themselves in so servile a position. It appears that towards the end of the century patrons had begun to feel the remuneration of their clients a burden, and to stint their sportula. Domitian even abolished the money payment for a time, and complaints are made that the good days for clients are over. The increased number of these dependants doubtless made the maintenance of the system difficult. The sportula was now demanded not only by poor and humble hangers-on of the great houses, but by persons of good position, so that Juvenal can even represent a consul adding up at the end of the year the income derived from his patron's presents. The satirist speaks with great truth and force of the demoralising effect of this universal parasitism. A man who is not ashamed to submit to the indignities which a client has to bear, does not deserve, he says, to be believed on oath in a court of justice. His patron is right to insult him : if a man will put up with anything he ought to be made to do so ; it is only a step further for the parasite to submit to a flogging like a slave. Better far to beg for bread on the mendicant's station than to be dependent on the liberality of some wealthy parvenu. Such, however, was not the opinion of very many people at Rome who thought it the highest boon of fortune to live at another's expense, and though ashamed to work, did not blush to live on charity.

The class below the majority of the clients was partly supported by humble occupations, partly dependent on the state-distribution of corn. This pernicious institution did more than anything else to undermine the health of the Roman community.

So far as we can learn, a very large number of persons resided in the capital simply in order to eat the bread of idleness, practising no trade, and addicted to all the vices which want of work never fails to encourage. These were the mob who frequented the public games and public baths, spending their whole day in a round of demoralising amusement, and preying upon the treasury, which in its turn could only supply the demand by exactions from the impoverished provinces.

We have now reached the lowest rung of the ladder, the class of beggars by profession. These were very numerous, a fact which perhaps testifies, as Mr. Lecky believes, to the generosity of the city in relieving distress. It appears, however, that in spite of the corn-distribution, a good deal of abject poverty existed at Rome, so that the beggars may have adopted their trade from necessity and not from choice. Some failed to secure their share of the dole, and food and everything else was dear at Rome. We are not surprised to hear of numbers of mendicants waiting about the bridges, the Servian Agger, and other places of public resort, making themselves regular stations there, sleeping on mats in the place where, in the day-time, they asked

for alms. Martial advises a destitute man to become a beggar rather than starve in honest indi-
gence; so, perhaps, some Roman mendicants obtained something more than bare subsistence.

Besides the broad division of the community
into three orders, and the subdivisions of the third
order according to the nature of their professions
or trades, social inequalities were largely fostered
by prejudices about race. Not only was the citizen
preferred to the non-citizen, the Italian to the
foreigner, but even the natives of other towns in
Italy were judged inferior to those who came of
Roman parentage. Augustus was reproached by
Marcus Antonius because his mother was a native
of Aricia. Livia Augusta was considered not to
be of unblemished descent, because her mater-
nal grandfather was a town councillor of Fundi.
Livia the younger, the wife of Drusus, son of
Tiberius, was seduced by Sejanus, upon which
Tacitus remarks, " So this woman, who was the
daughter-in-law of Tiberius and the niece of
Augustus, disgraced herself, her ancestors, and her
posterity by adultery with a *municipal*." Friedländer justly quotes this as one of the strongest
expressions of narrow Roman prejudice. And if

even the towns of Italy were despised by the
haughty natives of the capital, how much greater
was their scorn of provincials and foreigners! We
have already mentioned the disgust caused by the
Gaulish senators introduced by Julius Cæsar.
Cicero declares that the most distinguished Gaul
is not to be compared with the meanest Roman
citizen. Even the polished Greek was regarded
with hardly less disdain, a feeling in his case often
mingled with hatred at the superior adroitness
which enabled him to outstrip the slower or more
honest Roman. Umbricius* leaves Rome in disgust
and betakes himself to quiet Cumæ, because he
cannot bear to see Greeks put before him. " Shall
that man," he asks, " take precedence of me, who
came to Rome with a cargo of plums and figs?
Is it of no account that my infancy drew the breath
of the Aventine, and was nurtured on the Sabine
olive-berry?" How strange is the state of feeling
displayed by the invectives of the Augustan poets
against Antonius and Cleopatra! " Nefas, Ægyptia
conjux," " Dedecus Ægypti," " Fatale monstrum,"
" mulier ausa Jovi nostro latrantem opponere
Anubim." Such are a few of the expressions ap-

* Juv. Sat. 3.

plied to the Greek Queen of Egypt, the descendant
of a long and glorious line.   One might fancy
Cleopatra was a savage Æthiopian woman, who
had fascinated the representative of a princely
house. The fall of the Julian dynasty did something to modify this intense national pride.   First
Italians, then provincials, gained the imperial purple:
the sovereignty of the Roman stock was already
at an end, and the counterfeit which still survived
was less powerful and less exclusive. The empire
was gradually fusing all the different nationalities,
and breaking down the social distinctions which
the pride of a conquering race had so carefully
erected. The process was, however, very gradual,
for the "new men" were almost as tenacious of
their privileges and superiority as the old families,
and even the brilliant development of genius in
Spain during our period, and the splendour, rival-
ling Rome, of Antioch and Alexandria, failed to
compel the capital to recognise the provinces as
her equals.

There was, however, one exception to this rigid
exclusiveness, and that in a quarter where it might
have been least expected. The nobility of Rome
refused to treat the distinguished Spaniard or

Greek on a footing of equality, but they were often ready to court the wealthy freedman. Nothing in Roman history is more remarkable than the ease with which a manumitted slave passed into the privileged order, and obtained for his children and grandchildren, if not for himself, the same rights as genuine Romans, compared with the difficulties and restrictions thrown in the way of the free provincial who desired the same advantages. It may even be stated that a slave in a wealthy house at Rome had a better career open for his ambition than the ablest citizen of Antioch or Gades. Even in the matter of marriage, where aristocratic exclusiveness is generally strongest, the same curious phenomenon is displayed. The union of Antonius with the daughter of the Ptolemies was deemed a hideous disgrace : but Augustus found it necessary to make a law forbidding ladies of senatorial family to contract marriages with freedmen, and his successors at least often granted exemptions from it on the supplication of friends. The wife of Claudius Etruscus, a native of Smyrna, and slave of Tiberius, whose fortune it had been

"Semper Cæsareum coluisse latus,"

was the sister of a consul.* Antonius Felix, who,

* Stat. Silv. 3. 3.

in the words of Tacitus, " exercised the power of a king in the spirit of a slave," married Drusilla, the granddaughter of Antonius the triumvir. Such instances seem to have been common. In society such freedmen were not excluded from good circles, though their arrogance and bad manners often made them objects of hatred and disgust. The enormous wealth which they often possessed, of which we gave instances earlier in the chapter, was a sure passport to social success at Rome, where " everything had its price." A Zoilus, if he happened to be childless, was certain of plenty of deference and attention, even from the best families. His vices and vulgarities were more than compensated by his palaces and villas.

The vast majority of freedmen were, however, in a much more humble station. We find them in fact in every rank of life; in the learned professions, in trade, in commerce, in domestic offices, and in the lowest grades of poverty. From their numbers and position they gradually gave their type to the Roman community, which assumed more and more that de-nationalized and cosmopolitan character which ended in final disintegration.

We have yet to speak more in particular of some

of the foreign elements which had entered into Roman society, and we shall begin with the Jews, who, from their numbers and marked individuality, were a prominent feature in Roman society. So large was the number of Jews and Syrians in Rome that Juvenal complains that the Orontes has flowed into the Tiber. Josephus mentions 8,000 Jews established in the capital in his time. Seneca, in a fragment quoted by Augustine, declares that " the customs of that cursed race have prevailed so far that they are accepted over the whole world : the vanquished have given laws to their conquerors." Tiberius expelled 4,000 persons from Rome, and banished them to Sardinia, as infected with Jewish and Egyptian superstitions. Despised and hated as they were, they made many proselytes. From the establishment of the empire they began to push themselves into every class of society, and to exercise a powerful influence in the state. Caius probably learned his ideas of absolute monarchy from Herod : Titus was captivated by Berenice; and the number of converts to the Jewish faith cannot be counted. The Sabbath was a joke in Horace's time : in Juvenal's it was to many a reality. Outbreaks of persecution were sometimes sanctioned by the emperor : *e.g.* Tiberius expelled 4,000, as above-mentioned, and Domitian attacked the Jewish religion with a ferocity as great as that afterwards directed against the Christians. It is possible, as Merivale thinks, that the insurrection under Vespasian, and the destruction of Jerusalem by Titus, gave a death-blow to Jewish influence at Rome, but if so, it was not long before the progress of Christianity again made Jewish ideas an important factor in society.

Of other Oriental nations we may mention the Egyptians, who were celebrated for their skill in surgery, as well as for their licentious character, and the Syrians, who were much devoted to the study of astrology and kindred sciences. As for the Greeks, they pervaded the whole city and every class of society, so that Rome, in the words of the satirist, had become "a Greek city." The versatile Greek could turn his hand to every trade, from rhetoric to fortune-telling, and seldom allowed scruples to stand in the way of profit. It is not necessary here to enter further into the wide subject of Greek influence at Rome. The northern and western nations were very slightly represented among the free population, and their presence does not call for any special remark.

It still remains to speak of slavery, that most important of Roman institutions, and of the mass of human beings, probably exceeding in numbers all the rest of the population, whose legal position was simply that of chattels of the Roman people. In the chapter on morality we have already dealt with some aspects of the question, tracing the improvement in the condition of the slave which took place in our period, and the movement of public opinion with regard to humanity towards slaves. Here we must consider the slaves as one class in the community, and endeavour to present a complete though only outlined sketch of their life in that capacity.

Slaves were divided into two classes, the *familia urbana* and the *familia rustica*. The former consisted of domestic slaves, who performed all the duties of the household, the latter of the field-labourers on their master's country estates. Let us take first the domestic slaves, who were generally better treated and in a better position than the country slaves. The simple old custom by which a few slaves only were attached to the house, and ate at the same table with their master, had given place to immense crowds of domestic slaves, and a corresponding sub-division of labour. Wealthy Romans seem actually to have exercised their ingenuity in finding work for the largest possible number of slaves. It would be tedious to enumerate even a quarter of the offices which are mentioned in various Latin writers; among the most curious are the folder of clothes *(vestiplicus)*, the custodian of the Corinthian vases *(a Corinthiis)*, and the sandal-boy *(calceator)*, whose duty it was to put on his master's shoes. The management of this unwieldy and, perhaps, idle household, was committed to a head-slave, who held the post of *atriensis.* He was responsible for the good behaviour and industry of his subordinates, and allotted them their tasks. A large number were generally employed about the atrium, a large number in the kitchen, and a third detachment had its duties out of doors, to run errands, or attend their master abroad. Among these last we may notice as characteristic of Roman society the *nomenclator,* whose business it was to warn his master of the approach of any acquaintance and whisper to him the name, which he might otherwise have forgotten. Litter-carriers and simple attendants (*pedisequi*) were also in this class. In the house were the educated slaves, secretaries, librarians, readers, &c., and also the pages who waited at dinner, the dwarf, and the performers of various menial offices. We can find no parallel to the extraordinary multiplication of domestic slaves in the house of the rich Roman, unless it be in the effeminate luxury of an Oriental court. Parvenues were of course the worst offenders, men of the type of Zoilus, whose habits Martial describes in disgusting detail.* A gentleman and a man of self-respect would doubtless dispense with many of these ministers of self-indulgence and idleness. The *familia rustica* consisted of all the "hands" necessary to work the land and farm, ploughmen, keepers of horses oxen sheep mules pigs and asses, diggers, sowers, reapers, vine-dressers, gardeners, bee-keepers, gamekeepers, &c., &c., the whole number being usually under the superintendence of a *villicus* or bailiff, who appointed them their tasks, and distributed their rations. This class of slaves generally had a harder lot than the domestic slaves. They often worked in

* Mart. 3. 82.

L

chains, to prevent them from escaping, and at
night they were frequently huddled together in an
ergastulum, or barrack, half underground, which
must have caused great misery. It seems, from
Pliny and other writers, that in his time a more
merciful system was coming in.

How then was this immense demand for human
beings supplied?   In the first place, by the natural
birth of children in the slave-class.   The maxim of
the modern slave-dealer that it is cheaper to buy
than to breed, was not part of the Roman system
of economy. All writers on the subject recom-
mend that slaves should be encouraged to have
children, though they speak as if some owners
acted on a different principle. Columella even
recommends a "jus trium liberorum" to be granted
to "ancillæ," three sons conferring a claim to
"vacatio" or immunity from hand-labour, and a
greater number being rewarded by manumission.*
In general the "vernæ, ditis examen domus" were
undoubtedly regarded as a source of revenue.
They were not, however, the best servants, as they
were often forward and impertinent, and cunning
in evading their work. We have no means of

* Col. 1. 8. 19.

judging what proportion the *vernæ* bore to the
whole body of slaves, but in all probability the
birth-rate in the slave-class was low, and infant mortality very prevalent. Another source of
supply was opened by successful wars. It is probable that at one period of Roman history this
was the most fruitful recruiting ground of the slave
population. Whole nations were sold after a
victory, *sub hasta* or *sub corona*, according to
Roman phrase, this being the recognised treatment
of prisoners taken in war. But the empire was
less fertile in conquest, and other means had to be
resorted to. It appears that kidnapping was
carried on to a frightful extent. We even hear of
eastern provinces complaining that they can no
longer furnish their contingent of troops, the
population having been drained off by the slave-
dealers. A fearful picture is here opened before
us, and we regret that so little information is to be
obtained as to the extent of this iniquity and the
means by which it was carried on. We gather
that in out-of-the-way places, where the hand of
the law could not make itself felt, men were stolen
and carried off and sold as slaves, or shut up in
ergastula without a shadow of right. We are

astonished to find that this was the case even in
Italy, where Seneca declares that *ergastula
ingenuorum* existed, in which travellers and other
defenceless persons were immured. In Cicero's
speech pro Cluentio, a work in which nearly all
the blackest features of Roman life are collected,
we have an instance of a free man being kidnapped
and sold into slavery through the treachery of his
relations, who wished to get him out of the way.
This crime was probably not uncommon in an
age which invented the science of legacy-hunting;
and even without collusion on the part of the
relations it must have been extremely difficult for
the victim to escape or make the place of his
detention known to his friends. And if even
Italians were subject to this fate, what must have
been the case with the unhappy provincials, for
whom no one cared, when the greedy and unscrupulous *mangones* were ever on the watch to seize
some handsome boy or maiden for the Roman
market ?   If force was not possible, what could be
easier than to make a bargain with the tax-collector to distrain upon a poor family, and in
default of payment hand them over to the dealers ?
When we hear of the vast slave-marts at Delos

and other places, we cannot account for the numbers daily sold there, except on the supposition that immense numbers of free persons were illegally kidnapped and enslaved throughout the Empire. The existence of the Lex Fabia *de plagiariis* testifies to the prevalence of the crime ; but it is to be feared that where the pecuniary interests of the wealthy *mango* and the powerful purchaser were set against the claims of one who was at least *de facto* a slave, the chances of redress must have been slight indeed. The slaves who passed through the hands of the dealers were not all kidnapped. We hear of parents selling their children into slavery, and of poor persons voluntarily selling themselves. From what we said above on the subject of freedmen it may be imagined that in some cases an oppressed provincial might gain by entering the service of a Roman noble. Legal degradation to slavery was ordained in certain cases, the commonest probably being that of provincials who could not meet the demands of the tax-collector. Great cruelty and injustice probably resulted from this harsh usage.

The traffic in slaves was of course an important feature in Roman commerce. When a slave was to be sold, he was usually exposed on a platform (*catasta*), with chalked feet,* and a label round his neck setting forth his character, &c., and any faults he might have. If the vendor could give no warrant for him, a cap was placed on his head. The purchaser might bring an action for concealment of personal or moral defects. Sometimes, however, valuable slaves were sold privately, or in the back-rooms of shops, to avoid the curiosity of the vulgar, who could not purchase them. The prices of slaves of course varied widely. As luxury increased, the relative value of different sorts of slaves altered. A cook, who had formerly been the cheapest, was now (in our period) one of the dearest, of slaves. Ordinary field labourers were cheap—from £5 to £10 seems to have been an ordinary price for such. Skilled labour, of course, commanded a higher price, and *servi literati* sometimes fetched 100,000 sesterces, or even more. Instruments of vice and luxury were bought at extraordinary prices. We hear of 100,000, and even 200,000 sesterces being given for a *puer delicatus*, and 100,000 for a girl. Eunuchs fetched

---

* This was a sign that the slave had been brought from beyond seas.

immense sums, up to 500,000, and dwarfs, buffoons, and abortions of nature or art were much sought after. A trusted steward, *atriensis,* or *villicus,* would also command a high price. Of the nationalities, Greeks were naturally the most expensive, Sardinians and (probably) Syrians among the cheapest.

Great attention was given to the education of slaves for the place they were to occupy in the household. Those who were to exercise any handicraft were put to a careful apprenticeship ; those who were to amuse their master by jests and saucy repartees were given lessons in this art ; sometimes little *vernæ,* just emerging from infancy, were petted like dogs or kittens, wearing no clothes except coloured ribbons and gold and silver ornaments ; those who promised to be idiots were trained to improve their faculty for the amusement of their master, while those who shewed literary taste were trained as readers or secretaries ; classes generally consisting of ten were formed to facilitate the teaching of a large number, and houses called *pædagogia* were kept for those who were to serve as pages and cupbearers.

The treatment of slaves of course varied with

the character of the master. There are several
indications that their position was not altogether
so intolerable as some modern writers would have
us believe. The good old custom by which the
- *familia* dined at the same table with their master
had, it is true, ceased, as much from necessity as
from growing pride ; for the numbers were now
far too great for it to be maintained. We hear, however, that good masters always invited their slaves
to their *triclinium* during the Saturnalia, and on
feast days, and the system of rations had this
advantage for the slave, that he was able by self-
denial to save out of the allowance made to him,
and thus accumulate a sum with which he could
eventually hope to buy his freedom. The fact
that this was possible shews that the slaves were
not seriously stinted in the matter of food. The
peculium was indeed now universally recognised,
even in the *familia rustica,* and it was considered
a mark of recklessness and folly in a slave not to
have saved anything. Another pleasing feature
is the care taken not to divide families.* In
this respect Roman slavery compares favourably

* This subject has been spoken of already under the head of
" Morality." The repetition seemed unavoidable

with that of America in the present century, according to the best known accounts. The Digest rules that a legacy of a slave is to be taken to include his wife and children, "for it is not to be believed that he (the testator) meant to enjoin a cruel separation." Perhaps, however, we have no right to quote the Digest as evidence for the first century; and it may be reasonably doubted whether the obligation was recognised under the Twelve Cæsars. Some care seems, however, to have been taken about the *marriage* of slaves, if the term may be used where the law only recognized *contubernium.* Varro recommends that the slave and his wife shall be chosen to suit each other, though only apparently to make them work more contentedly.

The punishments of slaves will be dealt with in another place,* where we shall try to shew that a real though tardy improvement in humanity is perceptible through the period. We wish we could say the same of another subject, the most painful part of servile degradation. When Seneca says "Impudicitia in ingenuo crimen, in servo neces-

* We have, however, omitted the details of punishment and torture, which are not pleasant reading. Evidence is collected by Wallon, Becker, Marquardt, and others.

sitas, in liberto officium," we recognize how deep was the infamy to which slaves were often compelled to submit.* It is true that a magistrate already existed in Seneca's time whose duty it was to protect slaves from "sævitia et libido," but we fear the wrongs of the victims seldom reached his ears.

The most envied members of the servile class were naturally the official slaves of Cæsar's household, and those who held similar positions in the public offices. A *dispensator* of this class was quite a great man. An epitaph of a slave who held the office of *dispensator* of the imperial treasury in Gallia Lugdunensis, under Tiberius, has been found on the Appian-road. It mentions sixteen *vicarii* or slaves of his own who formed his escort at the time of his death. These gradations in rank were doubtless a great security to the masters, who could trust their upper slaves to keep the rest in order.

The feeling with which slaves were regarded was still very unsatisfactory. Stoic philosophers and men of refinement and humanity did their best to

* Lecky and Merivale both take too favourable a view of Roman morality on this head, but it is not necessary to say more about it here.

inculcate the natural equality of man; but a more
faithful indication of the popular opinion is given
by such cool classifications as that of Varro in the
preceding generation. "Agricultural implements
are divided into three classes—vocal, as slaves,
semi-vocal, as oxen, and dumb, as carts." The
"custom of our ancestors," always a potent force
at Rome, favoured this conception of the slave-
class, and it took some time for the more liberal
theory of the Stoa to win acceptance in the household and in the statute-book.

CHAPTER VII.

EDUCATION, MARRIAGE, &c.

In our last chapter we gave a short sketch of the component parts of Roman society. We shall now go through the life of the individual in the same way, considering in their order the chief points connected with childhood, education, marriage, and death. In this case also we shall have to be content with a brief summary of a very wide subject.

From the moment when he first saw the light, the Roman child was absolutely under the power of his father. As the family, with its sacred rites and continuous existence, was the unit of society, so the *pater familias* was the despotic head of the group he represented. As he had called his child into being, so it rested with him whether that being should be continued or not. A sickly or deformed child was generally drowned at once,*

* Sen. de Ira. 1. 15. 2.

and no obligation was felt to rear even a healthy
infant. If the question was decided in its favour,
the child was given one of the few *prænomina* in
use at Rome ; the sacred ceremony of lustration admitted him into the family circle ; the golden
token, the sign of free-birth, was hung round his
neck ; his birth was entered in the *acta diurna,*
and formal notice of the same given to the Prefect
of the Treasury. Still the father by no means lost
his authority over the person of the child. He
might punish him to any extent he liked, sell him
as a slave, or put him to death. The Romans of
our period recognised the anomaly of the *patria
potestas,* and noticed that it was peculiar to their
own code ; but they were very slow to modify it.
The customs of their ancestors were the foundation of their greatness : " Moribus antiquis stat
res Romana virisque," as old Ennius said, and it is
not till Hadrian's time that we find a man banished
for putting his son to death.

Education was begun at an early age. A boy
was first sent to a *litterator*—generally a slave or
freedman, who gave him a general instruction in
the elements of reading, writing, arithmetic, and
Greek. The next stage was the school of the

" grammarian," where the boy began to read standard authors in both languages, such as (in our period) Homer, Terence, Virgil, and Horace. Passages from these works were read aloud with the appropriate emphasis and intonation, and then learnt by heart. Questions were set on criticism, geography, mythology, and other subjects. Special attention was given to preparing the mind of the pupil for the next stage of his education, the lecture-room of the rhetorician. Suetonius tells us that at one time the grammarian used to teach rhetoric himself, but in our period he generally left that subject to professed *rhetors*, who received the boy after he had completed his school course. The discipline of the grammarians was severe, corporal punishment being freely applied to the idle and unruly. Holidays were long and frequent. Besides four months' vacation in the year, every feast-day and every market-day seems to have been a holiday, a system which approaches closely that of some of our public schools.

The physical side of education was not neglected. Games, as ball and other athletic exercises, were encouraged, the most approved being the old fashioned martial practice in the Campus. The

Greek *palæstra* had long since taken root in Rome, but it remained under the disapproval of those who preserved the old Roman feeling. The unpractical nature of the Greek training, the object of which was to develope beauty rather than to turn out good soldiers, was contrary to Roman theory; and the moral dangers to which the young were exposed in the *palæstra* gave a still stronger reason for the prejudice. Music and dancing were also distrusted by men of the old school, as derogatory to Roman *gravitas;* but both were taught to a large extent, and even girls learnt to dance. The sweeping assertion of Cicero, " Nemo saltat sobrius nisi forte insanit," will be familiar to most as an illustration of Roman feeling on this point.

On the moral training of the young we have very conflicting evidence. On the one hand we have such sentiments as Juvenal's often quoted " Maxima debetur pueris reverentia," and instances of careful enquiry as to the character of a tutor in Pliny the Younger and Quintilian; while on the other we have bitter complaints that these duties were not observed; that children were allowed to witness the vices of their parents, and that no care was taken as to the morals of their teachers, who were sometimes guilty of shameful abuse of their trust.

The toga prætexta, or robe of childhood, was laid aside for the ordinary dress of the adult citizen at about the age of fifteen. No definite age was fixed by law or custom, but the theory was, that the change should be made at the age of puberty. In fact it varied between twelve and eighteen.

The transfer of the boy from the grammarian to the rhetorician commonly took place before the assumption of the *toga virilis,* about the 14th year. It was in this third stage that the pupil was to prepare himself for the duties of active life. This was the aim of Roman education, practical here as in everything. Public speaking was the chief, almost the only, road to success in life for a citizen of the better class, and this was the subject to which he was now to devote his energies. Forensic oratory was not only the chief test of a man's accomplishments; it was of the utmost practical importance to every man of position at Rome.* Accordingly, the art was taught with a systematic seriousness unknown at the present day. The pupils were

* Cf. Tac. Dial. Or. 37, where he says, speaking of republican times, that no one could attain power without the help of eloquence.

instructed to study the best models, and to declaim against one another on given subjects, the master criticising and correcting the while. Rules of expression were formulated, and figures of speech carefully analysed and classified, so that oratory, instead of being left to the light of nature, as it now is, was raised into an exact science. Not that the pupil's whole time was occupied in learning the theory of rhetoric. A wide range of collateral subjects were studied for the sake of illustration, or simply to expand his mind. In particular, he generally attended the lectures of a philosopher, whose duty it was to teach him the springs of morality, and mould his character into a noble shape. It was hoped that the pupil would thus be led to think for himself, while his rhetorical studies would enable him to give just expression to the fruits of his meditations. But the tendency in our period was undoubtedly to give too exclusive an attention to rhetoric, the more practical side of education. Quintilian complains that "no sooner had the tongue become an instrument of profit than the study of morals was neglected, or left to weaker intellects;"*

* Quint. Inst. Orat. 1. 1.

M

and the same regrets are made by other writers. Too much declamation might doubtless be injurious; but if the due proportion was kept, the Roman system of education seems well conceived, and calculated to produce good men and useful citizens.

It was very common for young men to travel after completing their course of education at Rome. Athens, especially, was very often visited, and the lectures of philosophers and rhetoricians there were numerously attended. Among distinguished men who went to Athens in this way we may mention Cicero, Atticus, Horace, and Ovid.

The next event in the Roman's life which we have to consider is marriage. The ancient and venerable forms of *confarreatio* and *coemptio* had almost died out in our time; and most marriages were now mere civil contracts, dissoluble at pleasure. From the woman's point of view this loose form of alliance had considerable advantages. She did not pass into the *manus* of her husband, and retained the control over her property. Marriages were often contracted at a very early age. We hear of bridegrooms of sixteen, and of brides of twelve or thirteen. The ordinary age was from about 13 to 18 for girls, and from 20 to 30 for men. The

bride had little or no choice in the matter.
The bridegroom arranged the matter with the
girl's father in a formal contract by the words
"Spondesne?" "Spondeo." Friedländer points out
that the Latin language contains no word for to
ask in marriage. It is a little curious to find this
refusal of liberty of choice co-existing with the
freedom allowed to girls in other respects. They
were brought up in much the same way as boys,
learning, besides their own tasks of the distaff and
the loom, to read and write and study standard
authors under the eye of the grammarians. The
husband was, however, not much better off in this
respect. In most cases he knew nothing of his
wife's character till after marriage; often he had
hardly seen her till the contract was completed.
This unfortunate system, which has always been
characteristic of southern Europe, caused very
many ill-assorted unions and subsequent separa-
tions. It was not at all uncommon to betroth
mere children, even infants, to each other; the
imperial family affords several instances of this.

The day of marriage was celebrated at Rome, as
in almost all societies, by feasting and merriment.
The bride was arrayed in the marriage-veil and

girdled *tunica,* and her hair was arranged in six
ringlets. The gods were consulted by sacrifice and
the inspection of entrails; and the simple nuptial
ceremony was performed, after which a banquet
was held in the house of the bride's father. Then
followed the escorting of the bride to her new home,
where she was lifted over the threshold to avoid
the possibility of an ill-omened stumble, and the
ceremonies ended with the rude " Thalassio " song
outside the bridal chamber.

Marriage for the Roman woman meant a transition from rigid seclusion to almost unbounded
liberty. It is true that we hear of unmarried girls
attending the theatre and public spectacles, and
being present at banquets ; but these appear to be
exceptions due to the license of the age, and the
weight of evidence shows that great care was taken
to seclude the maiden from all that might injure
her innocence. In republican days a censor had
even punished a citizen of rank for kissing his wife
in the presence of his daughter. After marriage,
on the other hand, the greatest liberty was allowed
to the wife. She appeared, as a matter of course,
at her husband's table, whether he had company
or not; she could go where she liked, either to the

temples of Isis and Serapis or to the circus and amphitheatre; she had her own troop of slaves, over whom she ruled without interference; she could frequent the public baths; in short, no restraint was put upon her except such as her own modesty might dictate.

In our period this liberty was often disgracefully abused. It has been pointed out by more than one moralist, that in times of national corruption the women are generally more vicious even than the men. It was so at Rome. Not to mention the painful evidence furnished by Martial and Juvenal, the merē fact that we find such expressions as " cuius castitas pro exemplo habita est," speaks volumes for the corruption of society. But on this subject we need not here dwell. It is only necessary to mention it in order to explain that strange phenomenon of Roman life, the unexampled frequency of divorce. We are assured by Seneca that there were women in Rome who counted their age not by the consuls, but by their husbands, and by Juvenal that one had married eight husbands in five years. Divorce was resolved upon on the slightest pretext. Cicero put away Terentia apparently because he had a rich ward whose fortune he coveted; many separated merely from love of change, disdaining to give any reason, like Æmilius Paullus, who told his friends that " he knew best where his shoes pinched him." Passion and avarice were of course the most common motives.

Rich wives were not much sought after by wise men. Their complete emancipation made them difficult to manage, and many a henpecked husband acknowledged the truth of Martial's epigram—

> " Uxorem quare locupletem ducere nolim
> Quæritis? Uxori *nubere* nolo meæ,"

and exclaimed with Juvenal—

> " Intolerabilius nihil est quam femina dives."

Accordingly, since rich and poor wives were both objectionable, the large majority of men never married at all. So strong was the aversion from matrimony that neither taxes on bachelors nor rewards to fathers had any effect. In republican days a Metellus had expressed the common opinion when he said, " If, Romans, we could exist without a wife, we should all avoid the infliction, but since nature has ordained that we can neither be happy with a wife nor exist at all without one, let us sacrifice our own comfort to the good of our country." In the first century, A.D., men were less patriotic, but not a whit more disposed to married life.

Single or married, sooner or later death called away the Roman from his labours or enjoyments. Too often the last scene was hastened by over-indulgence. The reckless life which most men of fashion led was not conducive to longevity, and additional dangers beset the favourites of fortune in the avarice of a bad emperor or the impatience of greedy relations. But be the cause what it might, the end was to all the same : the eyes were closed by the nearest relation ; the cry (*concla-matio*) was raised to indicate that life had departed ; and the now lifeless corpse was laid out in the atrium of the house, arrayed in the toga, and often decked with costly ornaments. This was the care of the hired undertaker (*libitinarius*) and his assistant (*pollinctor*), whose duty it was to anoint the corpse and lay it out in the manner described. Every citizen* was clad in the toga

* Surely not "every free man," as Becker. The passage he quotes refers to voluntary disuse of the toga in their lifetime by *citizens.*

after death : the senator of course displayed his broad stripe, and the *triumphator* probably his *toga picta* or *palmata*. A chaplet of flowers was sometimes placed on the brow of the deceased. Nor did the Romans omit the dismal mockery of hired mourners. At the foot of the bed, wherever the body lay, sat two waiting women (*præficæ*) and a flute-player ; by the side stood three other mutes with dishevelled hair, beating their breasts in token of grief. These persons, the slaves of the undertaker, kept watch by the corpse during the greater part of the time which elapsed between the death and the burial. This time was commonly about three days.* During the interval, a branch of cypress was hung over the door or laid in front of it,† to indicate a house of mourning, lest any priest should incur defilement by entering it. At the end of this period the funeral ceremony took place. If the deceased was a distinguished man, a crier was sent, according to primitive custom, through the streets, with the words " This

* Another authority (Servius ad Æn. 5. 64) says seven days, which is unlikely. Perhaps, as with us, there was no fixed interval.

† Cf. Serv. ad Æn. 2. 714. Becker's translator says, " A cypress was planted near the house," which is absurd.

citizen is dead. If any one can come to the funeral, it is now time. He is being borne forth from his house." Meanwhile, the bier was carefully carried out of the door, feet foremost, and the strange procession set out on its way. First came a band of flute-players, whose piping made a funeral one of the noisiest things in Rome; then the female mourners already mentioned; next came—strange to say—a company of mimes and dancers, the leader of whom was dressed up to imitate the deceased. We cannot suppose that this class of persons was chosen merely as being likely to personate the deceased cleverly : there must have been an odd taste for the incongruity of comic actors taking part in a funeral profession. In fact, they were not expected to simulate grief, but often amused the spectators quite in the manner of their profession. The best story about them is given by Suetonius, when he is describing the splendid funeral of Vespasian, who had been notorious for his parsimony. During the proceedings the managers of the treasury were asked how much the funeral cost. They answered, " A hundred thousand pounds." " Give me a thousand only," cried the pseudo-Vespasian, and throw my

body into the Tiber!" Behind the mimes followed the procession of ancestors. The wax
masks, representing those of the deceased's family
who had filled any curule office, were taken down
from the niches in the hall where they usually
stood, and assumed by suitable persons, who also
put on the official robes of the magistrate whom
each represented; and thus attired—" the triumphator in his gold-embroidered, the censor in his
purple, and the consul in his purple-broidered robe,
with their lictors and the other insignia of office—
all in chariots, gave the final escort to the dead."*
The ceremony must have been half grotesque,
half imposing, the one feeling or the other predo-
minating according to the respect felt for the
deceased, and the management of the procession. Behind the ancestors came the corpse
itself, laid upon an elevated couch, richly adorned
with gold and purple. Pictures and effigies were
often carried after the corpse. Round the bier,
in their newly-donned caps of liberty, walked
the slaves whom the dead man had emanci-
pated by his will. These or the nearest relations of the deceased, often acted as bearers.

* Mommsen Hist. of Rome, 2. 395.

A crowd of friends and spectators followed the bier.

Thus the procession slowly proceeded to the Forum, where the bearers of the masks took their seats in the curule chairs, and the couch bearing the body was laid down. Then a friend or relation of the dead man pronounced the funeral oration, celebrating all the glories of his ancestors, and all the virtues for which he had been distinguished. The eulogy being ended, the procession resumed its course to the place of burial, which, by a law not always observed, was without the city-walls. There a pile of faggots and other combustible materials awaited them, on which the corpse was reverently laid. Then, while the waiting women set up a doleful noise, and the friends of the dead man threw offerings upon the pile, the nearest relation applied the torch, and the flame soon spread over the whole structure. During the burning it was not unusual for rich families to celebrate fights of gladiators. When the pile was burnt, the bones were carefully collected, sprinkled with wine and milk, then dried, and placed in an urn, with perfumes and unguents. The urn was then placed in the family sepulchre, which was generally by the side of one of the great roads just outside the walls. Formal words of parting were addressed to the deceased, and the company dispersed.

This is, of course, a description of the most splendid kind of funeral. It has been given at some length, as being perhaps the most characteristic picture of Roman life. We should add that the barbarous custom of supplying the dead man with the implements he used in life—ornaments, weapons, money, &c.—was largely observed, so that the interior of a family sepulchre sometimes resembled an ordinary dwelling-house. The poorer classes were content with much simpler obsequies. They often made use of " dove-cots," (*columbaria*), in which a niche received each urn. Burial clubs, which were very common, possessed these *columbaria*, and assigned places in them to their members. The lowest class of all—abject slaves and friendless outcasts—were, it is to be feared, often left unburied, or lightly covered with earth in the most hasty manner. Burial, as opposed to cremation, was not by any means unknown at Rome. Some families, *e. g.*, the patrician gens Cornelia, always practised it.

The funeral banquet consisted of two parts: first, the *silicernium*, which was held near the grave, and then the *cena novendialis*, which took place at the house of the dead man. Sacrifices and games were often held in his honour at the same time.

CHAPTER VIII.

—◆—

DAILY LIFE.

IT is an unfortunate necessity for any one who
tries to write about the habits and manners of the
Romans that he must confine himself almost
exclusively to the upper classes. Copious as are
the materials for the subject, they all bear on one
section of society. We can form a very clear idea
of most of the occupations and amusements of the
senator, the knight, and the millionaire ; but we
know next to nothing about the humble tradesman and poor client. The obscurity of low life is
scarcely illumined by a ray of light, either from
literature or monuments. It is a poor consolation
to say that this silence is itself highly characteristic ;
that the structure of Pagan civilisation was really
based on a foundation of crushed and forgotten
humanity ; we still wish to know how the despised
masses lived, the " leaches of the treasury," who
received their daily dole of bread from Govern-

ment, and carried their scanty earnings to the hospitable *popina*, with its savoury fumes of tripe and garlic. But our curiosity must remain unsatisfied. Rome has given us no Dickens to paint the trials and the humours of her slums for our instruction ; the empire did not even produce a second Plautus. Perhaps after all we have got what is most important. The life of the toiler cannot differ very much from one age to another. The dull routine of hard mechanical labour, the struggle for bare existence, the sordid amusements, were the lot of the inhabitants of the crowded Suburra, as of the East End of London. What we more miss is some account of the manners of the middle class, the respectable but not too successful tradesmen, the struggling professional men, and the small men of business. These classes have before now preserved a country from the fate which a corrupt aristocracy was bringing upon it ; and we should like to know whether they lived an honest and healthy life at Rome, amid the flood of vice and degradation around them. But the rich are in most respects the best representatives of a civilisa tion ; they have the opportunity of putting into practice the floating aspirations of the community,

and of employing for their own benefit the ingenuity and industry of the less-favoured classes.
Their habits are thus the best gauge of the attain-
ments of their country in civilisation, and of the
character which that civilisation has assumed.
Only we may be sure that a picture drawn from
the manners of the aristocracy is not better, but
worse, than the truth as regards the whole nation.
We in England should readily admit this. A
short time ago there appeared in a monthly
periodical an article entitled, "How the Rich live."
The description there given of the day of an idle
and wealthy English family bears a fairly close
resemblance to the records of the day of a Roman
noble, as collected from contemporary authors.
If anything, the first century seems to have the
advantage over the nineteenth, inasmuch as the
Roman professed to give some part of the morning to serious occupation, while the Englishman,
according to the writer in question, devotes the
short interval between breakfast and lunch to
sport or idleness. In gluttony the two seem
about on a par, the main part of the day in both
cases being given up to the pleasures of the table.
We feel how unjust and misleading such a descrip-

tion would be if exhibited as a picture of English civilisation as a whole. It is possible that gluttony may be a national temptation with us, but we should justly object to see it brought forward as our chief characteristic. Still more should we feel the injustice of leaving out of sight all our national virtues—our industry and integrity, and whatever else we love to credit ourselves with. Yet this is what we are obliged to do in the case of the Romans. The " daily life of the Romans " means the daily life of Atticus and Pliny, or of Apicius and Trimalchio. We can say nothing, because we know nothing, of the common-place but useful and industrious lives of humbler citizens. We shall do the Romans injustice, and imbibe false ideas ourselves, unless we remember that we are describing a small section of society, not the whole. Let us keep in mind the wide differences of habits which exist in our own community, and we shall then be less likely to join in the hasty and sweeping denunciations which have been poured upon Roman civilisation. An exclusive study of the manners of the aristocracy would, we admit, give a very false and unfavourable impression of the character of English society. Let us

N

remember that our knowledge of Roman life
confines us to a one-sided description of this kind,
and that it is no more true to say that the Roman
working-day was over by mid-day than that the
English day begins with a ten o'clock breakfast.
With this preparatory warning we will begin
to describe, as best we may, the course of the
Roman day.

An undisturbed night's rest was almost one of
the privileges of the rich at Rome. The owner of
a large mansion could place his bed-chamber out
of hearing of the streets. The rest of the citizens
had hardly composed themselves to rest after the
last diner-out and serenader had ceased to make
sleep impossible by their drunken songs and
doleful ditties, when the coin-stamper began to
hammer on his anvil, the schoolmaster to fulmi-
nate at his noisy class, and the hapless throng of
clients to hurry through the streets to pay their
respects to their patron. Those who had not to
perform this troublesome duty might consult their
own tastes as to the hour of rising. The elder
Pliny was usually at work by seven or eight, if not
earlier, but others might prefer to sleep off the
fumes of last night's Falernian till a much later

hour. Persius gives a not very pleasant picture
of a young gentleman of this kind whom his friend
finds still in bed near mid-day. It was the good
old custom for the household to meet at an early
hour for " family prayer," as we may call it. The
paterfamilias offered a sacrifice at the household
altar with his wife, children, and slaves standing
round. His clients and friends came in at this time
to pay their morning call, and the patron was
often willing to discuss their affairs with them, and
give them advice and assistance. This is the
pleasant side of the picture; in many cases the
" officia antelucana" were equally degrading to
patron and client.

At about nine the salutations were over, and
men who had any business to do began their
work. A large number found their way to the
Forum, either as pleaders, judges, or spectators in
the numerous law-suits: many went to attend a
marriage, funeral, sacrifice, or birth-day feast,
at a friend's house;* others set themselves to kill
time till dinner by dancing, dice-playing, drinking,
or other frivolous amusements; many betook

* For the engrossing character of these social duties, cf. Plin.
Ep. 1. 9.

themselves straight to one of the great public baths, or to the more manly exercises of the Campus Martius. Before setting out to any of these occupations it was usual to take a light meal called *jentaculum*, consisting generally of wine, dates, olives, cheese, &c., but sometimes also of meat.

The next event in the day was the *prandium* or mid-day meal, also called *merenda*, which was more like a substantial lunch than a breakfast, at least in rich households. It was followed by the siesta, which the climate of Italy made almost necessary. This generally lasted about an hour, after which most people took a bath.* This might take up the time till about three o'clock, when it was already not too early to think about the great event of the day, the *cena*.

We shall reserve some of the points connected with this meal for the chapter on luxury, for nowhere else did extravagance and self-indulgence shew themselves in so rampant a form. The *cena* was actually the last event of the day, beginning about three o'clock, and lasting till late evening, if not past midnight. Three hours was

* The baths are described in the chapter on Amusements.

apparently the shortest time that a rich man took over his dinner. But we must here remember what we said at the beginning of the chapter. The working man's dinner must have been a very different affair. We do not know whether he took it at the same time; if he did, we may be sure that his business called him back long before six o'clock. But the rich, as we said, remained at the table all the afternoon and evening. Hospitality was well kept up, so that it seems probable that it was the exception to dine alone. The ordinary number at a dinner party was nine. This was probably determined by the size of the tables and couches, three reclining on each of three sides, but the number has always been found a pleasant one for conversation. If a larger number were invited, more tables were prepared. The place of honour at table was *" imus in medio,"* the right-hand corner of the middle couch, while the host occupied the adjoining place *"summus in imo."* This gradation of places was part of the etiquette of the dinner table, which was carried to a great and indeed tiresome extent, so that a man unused to society found himself embarrassed and ridiculed for his ignorance of the rules of behaviour.

The absence of knives and forks made it difficult to eat gracefully, and the boor was recognized by the way in which he smeared his face and hands with the viands. A spoon was the only implement used by the guests, though the carver—a slave, of course—used a knife. Each guest brought a napkin to wipe his hands. The custom of reclining, with the left elbow resting on a cushion, was now universal for men; women and children sat, the position being considered more proper. This, however, like most customs founded on modesty, was often transgressed in our period. Round tables, called *sigmata*, were sometimes used in imperial times, the couches being then curved so as to fit them. These accommodated from five to eight persons. The invitations to dinner were sent by means of a slave called *vocator*, but the guests were often permitted to bring friends of their own, who were called *umbræ*. These inferior persons were usually relegated to the *imus lectus*. The guests came dressed in a festive attire called *synthesis*, the shape of which is not known. It was often of brilliant colours, scarlet, green, or purple, and ostentatious people sometimes changed it several times during an evening.

Of the materials of the banquet we hope to speak in another place; it consisted of three parts, the *promulsis* or *gustatio*, intended to whet the appetite and aid the digestion; the *cena* proper, which might consist of any number of courses from one to eight or more, and the dessert. The conversation during the meal commonly turned on the public spectacles, the comparative skill of famous gladiators, or jockeys, and the prospects of the different colours at the coming races. These topics were the more popular, as offering no handle to the treachery of the *delator*, who might take advantage of the festivity of the evening, and report an unguarded utterance as treason to the emperor.* Small talk might, however, flag during so long a meal; and accordingly it was usual to have music between or during the courses. Slaves were educated especially with the view to entertain guests in this way, and those who had

---

* Horace mentions, as a sample of small talk, "Thrax est gallina Syro par?" See also Mart. 1. 48.

> " De prasino conviva meus venetoque loquatur,
> Nec faciunt quemquam pocula nostra reum."

Paley takes this couplet in the opposite sense, as if the circus were the most *dangerous* topic of conversation; a view which seems very improbable.

none, hired musicians for the occasion. Martial, however, like Socrates, preferred a dinner without music. Dancing, rope-dancing, juggling, and jesting were also introduced for the amusement of the company, and not unfrequently the host took the opportunity of reading or reciting his own compositions to his guests, who felt that they were earning their dinner when they applauded each point in the tragedy or epic, written on both sides of the parchment, and even then not finished. Sometimes standard authors, or the last new popular poem, were read or recited, and this was probably the chief acquaintance with literature that the man of society obtained. The conversation, when it reached more serious topics than sport, was probably clever, ready, and sparkling. The constant intercourse of society and the method of education were both likely to produce wit and conversational power. The Romans had no newspapers, except the Acta Diurna, which was under government supervision, and they relied to a great extent on the talk of the dinner table to keep them supplied with the news of the day, the state of foreign politics, the newest domestic scandal, and the latest literary sensation. Conversation thus took the place of the daily press, the society journal, and the literary review. It was also made to do duty as a novel, and the "raconteurs," tellers of anecdotes, amusing "Milesian stories," and witty epigrams, were much sought after in society. The capital prided itself greatly on its sprightly humour, and the word *urbanitas* expresses the ready wit in which it excelled. Domitius Marsus wrote a book "*de Urbanitate*," which was probably a collection of good repartees, and rules for bringing them out. Other persons, who were not so gifted, might make it their business to collect the latest intelligence, and when occasion offered pour forth information from every province in the empire, like the telegram-column in our daily newspapers. These walking bulletins were not always much more appreciated than the meddlesome busybodies nicknamed "Ardeliones," who were among the pests of Roman society. It is to be feared that the retailers of scandal were more readily listened to, and that the talk of the dinner table was a dreaded danger to all who had a character to lose. License of speech and freedom from restraint were encouraged by the deep potations which accom-

panied the feast from the beginning to the end.
It was usual to drink in the Greek fashion, *i.e.*,
according to fixed rule, one of the party being
chosen (generally by dice) the master of the
revels, to settle how much wine was to be drunk,
and in what proportion it was to be mixed with
water. The wine was handed round by pages
generally selected for their beauty. It was prized
according to its kind and age. Setinian and
Cæcuban were accounted the best, then Falernian.
Some wine was preserved as long as a hundred
years or more, the date being attested by the label
on the bottle. Contests in drinking were not
uncommon, and a strong head was considered a
thing to be proud of.* Drinking of healths was
much practised, the guests generally pledging their
absent mistresses; these potations were sometimes
continued even till the morning light, and the

---

* Excessive drinking was a common vice at Rome, though the
wine of the ancients seems not to have produced such degrading
effects as beer and spirits. Pliny the Elder tells us a good deal
about the devices which were adopted to excite thirst : some. he
says, drank hemlock, that they might be obliged to drink wine to
save their lives ; others took pumice-stone powdered up. or other
doses. Tiberius went to see a man of Mediolanum, who could
swallow 17 pints at a draught. The emperor himself was no
mean proficient in the art, and his son Drusus inherited his
gifts.

peaceable citizen often had his slumbers broken by a reveller returning home.

So ended the day of the rich idler at Rome. In the country a simpler and more healthy way of life prevailed, but the same general plan was adhered to. Hospitality was not neglected in the country-houses, and birthdays, anniversaries, or religious festivals gave frequent excuses for entertainments. In the country a man had more opportunity for indulging his private tastes, and was less bound by the trammels of society. We have two interesting descriptions of the habits of men of rank and wealth but of high character, who were able thus to map out their day according to their own ideas. Pliny the Younger describes the life of Spurinna, an old man who had retired from active life. It was his custom to rise at seven, and walk three miles, the time being occupied by talking or reading aloud as he walked. Then after a short rest, with a book or conversation, he drove with his wife or a friend about seven miles. Next he walked again about a mile, then spent the time till two or three in writing. The hour for the bath was three in winter, two in summer. He prepared himself for it by walking naked in the sun, and by active exercise at ball. After the bath he rested and listened to light reading till dinner was announced (later, be it observed, than the ordinary hour at Rome), and this as usual occupied the rest of the day. By these habits, says Pliny, he had preserved his health and vigour till the age of seventy-seven. The other description we also owe to Pliny. It is that of the life of his uncle, the author of the "Natural History." Like Spurinna, Pliny was a very early riser, and when at Rome often visited Vespasian in the small hours, for he, too, used to work at night. Then he read and wrote till the time for the *siesta*, spending part of the time lying in the sun and taking notes from a book which was read to him. He bathed before the *siesta*, not at the usual time, and after it worked again till dinner time. During dinner a book was read, and the insatiable student even made notes between his mouthfuls. He rose early (*i.e.* before nightfall) from dinner, and apparently worked again. This extraordinary mode of life was carried on not only in the country but at Rome. Its results were seen in a perfect library of books on every subject, from physical science to rhetoric, from history to cavalry drill. We must be cautious of generalizing from such an exceptional character, but intellectual industry was a real feature of Roman civilisation, and many who never produced anything original took a superficial interest in literature, and devoted some hours every day to hearing books read aloud or attempting to write themselves.

CHAPTER IX.

AMUSEMENTS.

THE Roman populace, according to Juvenal, cared for only two things—Bread and the public shows. Without the former they could not exist; without the latter they would have felt their lives not worth living. The circus and the amphitheatre were indeed an absolute necessity, both to the people and to the government. To the people they furnished the means of passing idle days in pleasure and excitement; to the emperor they gave the opportunity of diverting the minds of his subjects from political affairs, and of supplying them with less dangerous food for rivalry and discussion. "Allow them, Cæsar," said Pylades, "to excite themselves about us, for then they do not think about politics."* It has been justly remarked that the spectacles under the Empire

* Macrob. 2. 7. Καὶ ἀχαριστεῖς, βασιλεῦ; ἔασον αὐτοὺς περὶ ἡμᾶς ἀσχολεῖσθαι, &c.

supplied to a great extent the place of the Comitia under the Republic. They gave the only opportunity for the citizens to meet together in the mass and express their opinions on any subject. At a time when literature was gagged, when political meetings and secret societies were alike suppressed, when even private speech was silenced by fear of the *delator*, there still remained the "license" of the circus and the amphitheatre, which enabled the Roman people to make its will known, and often to wrest compliance from a reluctant emperor. The shouts of the assembled thousands, carefully organised beforehand, on several occasions procured the revocation of an unpopular edict, or the punishment of a hated minister. Even Tiberius was induced by the shouts of the people to restore a statue which he had removed from the baths of Agrippa and set up in his own palace.* The Emperors were not always, however, so compliant. Augustus refused to repeal his marriage law in deference to the popular clamour, and Caius even seized and put to death the ringleaders of a similar demonstration. In general, however, no restrictions were put upon

* Plin. H. N. 34. 62.

this license, which seems to have increased in the later period of the empire. Tertullian, for instance, speaks of ridicule and abuse directed against the Emperor himself, as a common occurrence at the games; but of this we find no trace in the first century. These demonstrations were, as we have said, organized beforehand, and it stands to reason that, in cases where the people were not of one mind, rival shouts, each trying to drown the other, were raised from different sides. Sometimes the government tried to utilize the custom for its own purposes. Titus is said to have hired persons to demand in the theatre the death of men whom he suspected and wished to get rid of.* Private malice was sometimes indulged by shouting scandalous insinuations at the games, and this was punished as a very malicious form of libel.

But if the spectacles were a political necessity, they played a far more important part as the amusement of an idle population. How much space they filled in the life of the metropolis may be estimated when we enumerate the various feasts on which they were given. The number of

---

* Suet. Tit. 6. Titus, however, was not yet emperor when he did this.

these holidays was constantly increasing. Under Tiberius it had already reached eighty-seven days, and before the end of the century it probably exceeded one hundred. But these numbers only represent the regular festival-days. There were also the extraordinary fêtes, which occurred very frequently, and were sometimes prolonged to an inordinate length of time. Thus the opening of the Colosseum was celebrated by a fête of one hundred days, and Trajan, in 106, gave one which lasted one hundred and twenty-three days. In the time of Aurelius the *dies fasti* had been reduced to two hundred and thirty. Such was the life which the rulers of the world chose for themselves, and which the subject provinces had to support by the fruits of their labour.*

The spectacles which were enacted on these numerous holidays were principally of three kinds. First in importance, and for a long time in popularity, were the combats of gladiators and wild beasts in the arena. Next were the horse races in

---

* The frequency of spectacles, of course, varied in different reigns. Tiberius is said never to have given a show of gladiators himself, and to have rarely attended such exhibitions. Hence the rush to see the spectacle at Fidena, given by Atilius, a freedman, which led to the disaster there.

O

the circus, which at last evoked even more enthusiasm than the "games" of the amphitheatre. And lastly the dramatic exhibitions, which, in the degraded form of pantomime, were almost as popular as the fiercer forms of entertainment. To these must be added the varied class of street entertainments, such as mountebanks, jugglers, and street musicians; and the illuminations which were given in honour of special occasions. This last class will not require much space; but the three great entertainments of the arena, the circus, and the theatre, call for more detailed attention.

Of the gladiatorial shows, which we shall consider first, we have already spoken in a former chapter. The remarks we then made were directed to the moral effects of this singular institution, and to the indications which it gives of the state of feeling then prevailing on the subject of humanity. We shall now approach the same subject from a different point of view, and consider the games of the amphitheatre as one of the three great amusements of the Roman populace.

The origin and early history of the games need not detain us. The tradition which ascribes their invention to Etruria is supported by evidence, and we may regard it as certain that this was one of the evil legacies that Rome inherited by the absorption of their peculiar people. In the beginning of our period they had already gained immense popularity, and were spreading over the provinces, till even Greece, which had long refused to tolerate them, boasted its amphitheatre.

The combatants in the arena belonged to four classes—slaves, prisoners of war, condemned criminals, and free men who voluntarily entered the profession. The exposure of slaves was eventually forbidden. That of prisoners was justified by the harsh law of antiquity. Criminals were condemned to fight, as an aggravation of the capital sentence, for no discharge or quarter was allowed them.* It was sometimes suspected that innocent persons were occasionally condemned to this punishment in order to make up the number of combatants, and when we hear of 300 criminals exposed at one time, it must be confessed that there were grounds for the suspicion. The fourth class of volunteers was composed of various elements. Libertines who had exhausted their

* A popular prince would, however, sometimes grant even a criminal to the request of the populace. Suet. Ner. 12.

O 2

fortunes, inexperienced young men who were inveigled into joining a school of gladiators, desperadoes of all kinds, submitted themselves to the stern discipline of the *lanistæ*, and took the oath which bound them to submit to be burnt alive, beaten, or killed with the sword at the bidding of the trainer. Some embraced the profession from mere love of fighting or of notoriety,* and the rewards which could be won by a successful swordsman were enough to tempt even the ambitious.

The training through which the gladiator went was methodical and severe. He was hardened to bear pain by being beaten with rods and whips. His diet was regulated with a view to increase to the utmost his strength and activity. He was constantly practised in the use of the weapons he was to use in the arena, and great attention was paid to bearing and deportment, which were almost as much criticised as skill in fencing. On the day of the combat he was attired in splendid armour and furnished with richly adorned weapons; nothing was omitted which could add to the effect

---

* Lucian introduces a story of a Scythian who offered himself as a gladiator in order to earn 10,000 sesterces to help a friend in distress.

of his appearance, or enhance the brilliance of the show. The expense of all this preparation and equipment fell ultimately on the giver of the games, who was either the emperor, or an aspirant to public office, or sometimes (especially in the country towns) a wealthy parvenu. Some rich men kept gladiators of their own, and these, on more than one occasion, displayed a fidelity and devotion to their master which fills us with surprise. The cost of a show was, of course, immense, and was felt to be a burden even by the wealthy Roman aristocracy. Many able men were debarred from public life through their inability or unwillingness to incur the expense ; and at last (though not in our century) it became difficult to find qualified persons to take the highest magistracies. A great part of the money passed through the hands of the *lanistæ,* who often contrived to make large fortunes out of their disreputable trade.* Large salaries were also paid to celebrated swordsmen, and handsome presents were given them besides their regular pay. Sometimes "*rudiarii,*" or discharged gladiators, were induced to re-enter the arena for

* Cf. Mart. 11. 63.

a large sum.* When we consider the expense of providing wild beasts from Asia and Africa,† and the presents which were often scattered broadcast among the spectators, we are almost disposed to wonder that private fortunes could ever endure such a drain.

The social position of the gladiator bore some resemblance to that of the jockey in some circles of modern England. His trade was always considered a mean one, but the passion for sport raised the successful performer into a hero, so that the champion *"secutor"* or *"retiarius"* divided with the heroes of the circus the honour of being more talked about than any one else in Rome. The stigma, however, still remained. It was rare for the sons of gladiators, even when rich, to hold official positions; and those who left the arena without having saved money often sank to the lowest depth of poverty and misery.

It is not difficult to conjure up a picture of the Colosseum on a festival day. 80,000 human beings

---

* Tiberius (Suet. Tib. 7) paid 100,000 sesterces a piece to *rudiarii* to induce them to fight in one of his spectacles.

† This, however, generally fell on the provincials, who were forced to contribute animals for the games under the name of *vectigal aedilicium.*

are there assembled in their holiday attire, the
citizens crowned with garlands and in white robes,
the senators with their broad purple stripe, and
behind them the motley crowd of all nations and
costumes, the vestals in their seat of honour next
to the arena, the emperor with his suite in the
podium, — all sit intent on the brilliant scenes
enacted in the centre of the vast building, scenes
varied by every device of art and ingenuity, and
continued in an unbroken succession from sunrise
to sunset.   Now a duel between a *" secutor "* and
a *" retiarius,"* produces splendid feats of agility
and dexterity; now the *"parmularii"* and the
adherents of the larger shield " back " their re-
spective factions with clamorous shouts ; now the
arena is suddenly filled by troops of armed men, who,
concealed in vaults beneath, seem to rise by magic
from the earth; now a crowd of savage beasts —
captured, some in the Soudan, some in Central Asia,
some in the wild regions of the north — are let loose
to fight and kill each other : now some wretched
criminal is exposed, tied to a stake, to be lacerated
by a bear or a bull, or burnt in the *tunica molesta ;*
now Scævola, in the person of an unhappy male-
factor, allows his right hand to be consumed in

the "Tuscan fire"; now the whole arena is sub-
merged, and a sea-fight enacted with all the picturesque evolutions of ancient naval warfare. Such
were some of the exhibitions which captivated the
Roman populace. We shudder at the cruelty, but
we can well understand the terrible fascination
which such spectacles must have exerted.

The Great Circus, which filled the valley between
the Palatine and Aventine Hills, was probably the
most stupendous building ever erected for public
spectacles. It held at different periods 150,000,
250,000, and lastly 380,000 spectators, the second
of these figures referring to the time of Titus, and
the last to the fourth century. The space enclosed
by this enormous structure was used for several
purposes. Besides the horse races, which were
the main entertainment provided for those who
attended the circus, gladiatorial combats on a large
scale were performed there, and sometimes athletic
contests were held in the circus instead of in the
stadia built for the purpose. But the chariot races
were the main attraction, and it was for these that
the arrangements of the circus were designed. All
round the course tiers of seats rose one behind
the other to a great height, the *pulvinar* of the

emperor being placed in the most advantageous position for seeing both the beginning and the end of the race. Down the middle of the course ran the *spina*, a low wall with *metæ* or turning posts at each end, these last being composed of three conical pillars set on a pedestal.* The number of rounds run was registered by the simple contrivance of seven balls, one of which was placed on† the *spina* at the end of each "lap". The stalls where the horses were kept were at one end of the course, behind the starting point. The racecourse had this advantage over ours in England, that the spectators never lost sight of the horses, which came round and round several times before the end of the race. It is difficult to imagine any spectacle more exciting to a frivolous populace than these *circenses*. From sunrise to sunset, day after day during festivals, which sometimes lasted from one week to another, the Roman people could regale themselves with a ceaseless succession of chariot races. We hear of twelve, and even of twenty-four courses being run in a single day, the latter being apparently the more usual number ; and

* Metasque imitata cupressus. Ov. M. 10. 106.
† Or, perhaps, *taken off* it. Varro R. R. 1. 2. § 11.

when we reflect on the length of the course, which
was ordinarily seven times round the circus, we
are forced to the conclusion that not less than
twelve hours of the day must sometimes have been
taken up by the actual races, without making
any allowance for intervals.* It was, however,
usual to allow four intervals, the principal at mid-
day, during which the spectators might retire for
refreshment or short exercise. I am not aware
that we hear of any arrangement corresponding to
our "keeping places," though we know that the
struggle for good seats was very keen, and that the
crowds were wont to assemble many hours before
the races began : but we hear of *locarii* being paid
to take seats beforehand for those who could not
come early, and possibly spectators employed their
slaves to prevent others from occupying their
places during their absence. The interest of the
races was not confined to trials of speed among

* Friedländer calculates the length of the course at 7½ kil.,
and the time occupied by each race at, at least, half-an-hour. I
am disposed to regard this last estimate as rather too high, for we
hear, as he tells us himself, of 48 courses being run in a single day
on an exceptional occasion, a feat scarcely compatible with this
estimate of time, even if we adopt his supposition that the length
of the courses was shortened on this occasion. Guhl and Koner
estimate 25 minutes as the duration of a race.

the horses. Skill and chance both played an important part, and the danger which attended every race added zest to the enjoyment of the spectators. The reliefs, and other representations of races which have come down to us, nearly all represent chariots overturned and men and horses struggling in wild confusion on the ground. Such accidents must have been very frequent in rounding the sharp turn at the end of the *spina*, and we are not surprised to hear of dangerous and even fatal accidents suffered by the drivers. But the main excitement was due to the existence of factions pledged to favour one of the four parties into which the competitors were divided. These parties were named after four colours, red, white, blue, and green, and every charioteer was attached to one of these parties, and wore its colours on the day of the race. Two of the colours, the red and the white, were eclipsed during our period by the other two, so that the chief rivalry was between the blues and the greens. These two colours divided, one may say, the whole population of Rome, and produced as keen a rivalry and party spirit as had ever been evoked by the constitutional struggles of better days. This monstrous absurdity was

growing rapidly during the whole of the first century, but it did not reach its height till long after.
It was reserved for the new Rome of Constantine
to see its streets deluged with the blood of its
citizens slain in tumults excited by these coloured
rags.*   In our period the evil, though great enough,
did not reach gigantic proportions. The Romans
of the early Empire were generally content to shew
their interest in their party by lavish expenditure
on training, by extravagant rewards to drivers who
had led their colours to victory, and by exalting
Scopus and Incitatus and Andræmon to a celebrity
which the most popular poets could not hope to
rival. The drivers could make, Juvenal says, as
much money as a hundred advocates, and if they
escaped being crushed or dashed to pieces on the
racecourse, might look forward to a comfortable
retirement after a few years of danger, excitement,
and notoriety. Their social position, though higher
than that of the gladiator, was still a low one. Most
of them were either slaves, or of the rank just
above slavery; and it was considered highly disreputable for a Roman citizen of rank to exhibit

---

* The Nika sedition. in which 30,000 persons are said to have
perished, is described with great power by Gibbon, ch. 40.

himself in the costume of a jockey. So great, however, was the enthusiasm evoked by the racecourse that even senators and knights could not be restrained from appearing in the circus. When we remember the manner in which Juvenal speaks of a consul who drove his own carriage on the high road, we can form some idea of the scandal which this practice caused, and the mischief which the degradation of the upper classes in the racecourse, as in the arena, inflicted on society in general. When a Roman lost his sense of dignity and self-respect he lost that which produced the best features of his character, and probably nothing did more to break the ties of nationality in the city than the shameless participation of some of the nobility in these spectacles. Except for this, we cannot regard the circus as an altogether pernicious institution, considering the condition of the population of Rome. It did harm, no doubt, in fostering the idleness to which they were prone, but it may be questioned whether, if the races had not existed to act as a safety valve for the popular factiousness, graver political dangers might not have arisen. At all events, in so far as they outbid in popularity the far more horrible and degrading shows of the amphitheatre, we may admit that they did some service.

It might be supposed that the enthusiasm which the gladiatorial games and the races of the circus excited among the people left them no time for other amusements. But though the theatre never quite rivalled either of these in popularity, the Romans of the first century were very far from indifferent to this form of entertainment. On the contrary, they found time amid their other diversions to take a very strong interest in dramatic exhibitions, and even to extend to favourite actors some of the partisan spirit which they shewed to distinguished jockeys and gladiators. The theatre always remained a highly important feature in Roman life.

There is, perhaps, no better indication of the character of a nation than its stage. In our own history, the drama of the Elizabethan era, of the Restoration, and of the present day, all present a faithful image of the current taste of the time to which they belong. The same may be said of the modern French drama. We shall therefore approach the subject of the Roman stage with great interest, as one of the most important portions of our subject. The taste of the people in dramatic exhibitions will enable us to lay our finger on more than one of the salient features of their social life.

Suetonius speaks of three theatres in Rome.* They were called after Pompey, Balbus, and Marcellus, and probably held from 50,000 to 80,000 spectators. They were arranged in the form of a semicircle, with rows of seats rising to a great height, so as to accommodate the greatest possible number of spectators. The size of the theatre must, however, have made hearing difficult, and placed genuine drama at a disadvantage. Perhaps the popularity of the *mimes*, of which we shall speak presently, was partly due to this. Gesticulation may be seen and appreciated where dialogue can be only imperfectly heard.

The old Atellan farce still maintained its popularity among the lower classes. The well-known characters — Maccus, the amorous old scoundrel; Dossennus the swindling soothsayer; Bucco, the babbling fool, still exhibited their familiar characteristics in new and old combinations. These prototypes of the Italian comedy of the middle ages,

* Suet. Aug. 44.

and of our modern pantomime, were always popular with the masses at Rome, whose tastes were further consulted by a large admixture of grossness and ribaldry in the performance. The mime, properly so called, seems to have differed only slightly from the Atellan farce. It admitted, however, a somewhat wider field of subjects, and thus enabled the playwright to spice his drama with profanity as well as indecency, or to horrify his audience by skilful imitations of scenes of torture. The accounts we possess of these representations seem to indicate an extremely low and degraded taste on the part of the populace. Such intellectual pleasure as was sought was derived chiefly from audacious sallies against the first principles of morality, or from jests directed against the gods; while the plot generally turned, as in French fiction of the present day, on the successful violation of the marriage tie and the discomfiture of the injured husband. But the main attraction of the mime was even a lower one than this. That shameless freedom of speech, which Martial, himself one of the greatest offenders against decency, praises as " Romana simplicitas," was here exercised to its fullest extent, and even the eyes were gratified by the most disgraceful exhibitions under pretext of the license of the Floralia.*

It is necessary to say thus much on the subject, because a profane and immoral stage is, as we have said, a sure sign of an irreligious and corrupt society, and it is impossible to omit so important a feature in the life of the epoch. There was, however, another use to which the mimes were put. We have already mentioned the license taken by the assembled people in the circus and amphitheatre of expressing their wishes in the presence of the emperor if they wanted any law repealed or unpopular minister punished. We said then that disrespectful cries directed against the emperor himself were almost unknown in the first century, though common afterwards. But the Roman people needed some means of satirising their rulers, and, as even the " *licentia circi* " had its limits, some other and less direct way had to be found for expressing what could not be said openly. This was found in the mimes and farces. An allusion, however guarded, to the emperor's

* Ovid, Tristia 2. 497–520, pleads vigorously and not unreasonably against the inconsistency which condemned so severely his own erotic poetry, while it tolerated the more mischievous grossness of the stage.

P

personal habits or conduct was at once caught up and loudly applauded by the audience. So customary was this species of innuendo that the most innocent-sounding lines might be taken as covert allusions to scandals, which it would have been treason to speak of, and the author might thus shelter himself under the plain meaning 'of his words. This kind of ingenuity was especially suited to the Italian mind, and was exercised not only in the theatre, but in the court of justice. For instance, Cicero tells us that on one occasion the court seized on the number 53, which a witness gave as the distance in miles of his farm from Rome, shouting " Ipsa sunt," remembering, he says, that this was the amount of money he had taken as a bribe. These allusions were introduced into the Atellan farce as well as into the mimes. They were not without danger to the author and actor. A luckless poet was burnt alive by Caligula for a line which seemed to contain a covert jest on himself, and an actor was banished from Italy by Nero for a like offence. Helvidius Priscus, the younger, was executed by Domitian for a play which seemed to allude to the emperor's recent divorce.

The popularity of these indecent exhibitions, which had formerly been patronized only by the vulgar, was the subject of constant complaints by the prætors.* Tiberius, in one of those ebullitions of high-handed morality with which we are familiar in ancient and especially in Roman history, issued an edict expelling all players from Italy. This, however, probably belonged to that class of prohibitory edicts, which, as Tacitus says, were always being issued and never really enforced. It was impossible to deprive the people of so popular an amusement. The law seems to have been repealed by Caligula, and reissued at least once before the end of the century.

The subject of these dramas, if they deserve the name, was often mythological, seldom historical, generally amatory. It was common to take some legend which contained materials for erotic scenes, and to elaborate them to suit the popular taste. The writers of the plays were generally men of small literary capacity; but sometimes good poets, such as Lucan and Statius, did not disdain to turn their hand to this species of composition. We also hear of adaptations from existing works. For

* Tac. Ann. 4. 14.

instance, scenes from Ovid, very likely from the Metamorphoses, were introduced in the mime.

A large part of the art of the pantomime consisted in dancing. The dance was, however, as much the work of the arms and of the whole body as of the feet. It was accompanied by gesticulation, which was brought to such perfection that in the pantomime proper the help of words and even of music was dispensed with, and the whole scene enacted in dumb show. If this surprises us, we must remember that the Italians have always been celebrated for their use of gestures. At Naples, at the present day, every emotion has its appropriate sign, and the inhabitants can convey the expression of their admiration, defiance, or any other feeling, by the use of the hand only. The same custom prevailed at Rome, as is shewn, amongst other things, by the interesting description in Plautus (Miles Gloriosus, Act 2, Scene 2) of a man engaged in deliberation with himself. The pantomimes further elaborated this system of signs, so that a clever actor had no difficulty in carrying his audience with him. The system had this advantage that the language of signs is common to all nations, while the actor was generally a Greek or

Egyptian, and his audience, perhaps, a motley crowd from all nations of the empire. The chief requisites for success in a pantomime were a handsome and well-formed person, grace of movement, and power of adapting himself to any part, including those of women. The most celebrated dancers, Pylades and Bathyllus, possessed these attributes to perfection, and succeeding artists were accustomed to take their names as an assumption of championship in the profession. It was usual for an actor to take more than one part, sometimes without changing his mask ; but this was probably exceptional, and merely an exhibition of versatility.

The social position of the actor or dancer resembled somewhat that of the circus driver. Roman tradition was very strong against allowing actors any social status at all. They long regarded all such professions with the same contempt that Englishmen until lately felt for them.*

The law was called in to impose ignominious penalties on an actor who intruded in any way

* See an amusing passage in one of Lord Chesterfield's letters : "If you are fond of music it is well: get a Frenchman or an Italian to twang and whistle to you ; but never let me see you with a pipe in your mouth, or a fiddle under your chin."

into the classes above him.   Corporal punishment
was freely employed upon his person.   He was
ranked with slaves and barbarians.   Any Roman
citizen who appeared on the stage, except in an
Atellan farce, was liable to be adjudged *infamis*.
As a natural consequence he generally was a slave
or freedman, or a native of some country where
his profession was more esteemed, such as the
Greek colonies and the East generally.   His
notoriety did not do much towards raising his
legal status, though in some cases a brilliant actor
won for himself a distinguished position in actual
life, and accumulated a large fortune.   He might
rise to high favour at Court, and hope for large
presents in money from the emperor.   In many
cases he would attach himself to the imperial
troupe, which was generally the best in Rome.
In this way even political power was not out of
his reach, and socially he might hold a brilliant
position, and be courted by senators and magistrates.   In spite of this, however, his profession
always remained under a ban ; and should his
popularity cease he might find himself reduced to
a position little better than that of an ordinary
slave.

The mime and the Atellan farce were so much the most important kinds of dramatic exhibition that we need not detain ourselves long with the higher kinds of entertainment. The *palliatæ* or Greek comedies lingered on without much success ; tragedy was moribund, and only resuscitated by the help of brilliant scenery and imposing names, in the style of modern Shakespeare revivals. Tragedies were, indeed, written by hundreds ; but they were not intended for the stage, and the personal friends of the author were usually his reluctant auditors.

Among the minor spectacles the most important were the athletic contests, commonly exhibited, as we said above, in *stadia* prepared for the purpose, but sometimes in the circus. It was a long time before these Greek amusements naturalized themselves on Roman soil, and in our period they excited a comparatively languid interest, though some emperors encouraged them. The contests were arranged in *Quinquertia*, in imitation of the Greek Pentathlon, and consisted of running, leaping, wrestling or boxing, throwing the quoit, and the javelin. We may also mention here the fêtes and illuminations, generally accompanied by presents to be scrambled for by the crowd, which served to amuse the populace in the intervals of more serious spectacles.*

The transition from public exhibitions to the bath is not so great as may at first appear. The public bath ought certainly to be classed among the amusements of the Roman populace. It occupied a very large amount of time in the life of every citizen, and perhaps the greater number indulged in it every day. This luxury was a late product of Roman civilisation. The primitive Romans only took a bath on market-days,† contenting themselves with more partial ablutions in the meantime. At the end of the republic more luxurious manners had come in. It was already the custom to bathe for pleasure rather than for cleanliness, and a bath-room was already a necessary adjunct of every large house. Public baths on a humble scale were already numerous. These were probably private speculations, and the price of admission was a *quadrans*. Agrippa

---

* These *sparsiones* formed a regular part of the circenses. A refinement was to throw, not the presents themselves, but numbered tickets, which entitled the possessor to a prize, sometimes of considerable value.

† Sen. Ep. 86.

was the first to introduce one of those splendid structures which afterwards occupied no small part of the city of Rome. These *thermæ* were provided not only with air and water baths of every kind, but included gymnasia, *exedræ*, or lecture rooms for poets and rhetoricians, walks and plantations, fountains and statues, ball-courts, vestibules, porticoes, and probably libraries— everything in fact that the bathers could want to amuse them after the bath or prepare them for it. It is perhaps worth noticing that the example of Agrippa was not followed for a whole generation, the next *thermæ* being those of Nero. Merivale suggests that the greater publicity of the thermæ offended the dignity of the Roman, who was still ashamed to strip in public except for the actual bath. If this feeling still existed under Augustus, it certainly disappeared very quickly, and before the end of the century the thermæ became a most important and popular institution at Rome. Of the magnificence of these buildings it is impossible to speak too highly. The 86th letter of Seneca gives a glowing description of the plebeian's bath. The walls blazed, he tells us, with precious marbles, the chambers were adorned

on every side with gorgeous mosaics, the water
was discharged from silver taps into marble basins
—in fact, he adds with rhetorical hyperbole, our
feet disdain to tread except on precious stones.
It is well to try to form a mental conception of
such a building, surpassing, probably, in magnificence anything that Europe has now to show, and
then to remember that there were several of these
establishments in the capital, and all of them open
to the meanest citizen on payment of the smallest
coin in the currency, or in many cases, absolutely
gratis.*

The Romans were not slow to avail themselves
of the advantages thus thrown open to them. We
hear of persons bathing as many as seven times a
day,† and a daily bath was, as we have said, the
rule. The afternoon was the usual time of the
day; and Hadrian even forbade any except invalids
to bathe before two o'clock.‡ The courts of the

---

* It was a common act of liberality to throw open a bath free
for one day, or longer. This was sometimes provided by will,
e.g., Agrippa, Dion. 54. 29.

† Becker is hardly justified in his stricture on Gell for this
statement. Besides Commodus, Gordian and Gallienus are said
to have bathed seven times a day, and no doubt they had imitators
in a humble position. Remmius Palæmon, in our period, bathed
"*sæpius* in die." Suet. de Gr. 23.

‡ Spart. Hadr. 22.

thermæ were filled with loungers, and the *exedræ* with ambitious declaimers and poets, who victimised the indolent bathers by reciting to them their compositions. The moral effects of this excess were, of course, highly pernicious. Besides the enervating effect of the bath itself, the decent rules which forbade the young to bathe with the mature, and those which prevented the two sexes from bathing together, were relaxed; till in the latter half of the century, it was quite common for men and women to make appointments to meet each other in the bath. It stands to reason that this was not done by respectable women, but the frequent mention of legislation on the subject shews how difficult the practice was to eradicate. In most cases the women either had separate rooms, or were admitted at different times to the men. Some bathing dress was worn by the women, but not by the men.

Besides the baths at Rome, the use of mineral springs and health resorts was known to the Romans. Very few of the places which are now frequented by invalids within the limits of the empire escaped their notice. In Italy itself several places were visited for the sake of their baths. The chief seem to have been Puteoli, Sinuessa,

Linternum, and above all, Baiæ.*   Baiæ became a
centre of fashionable life and amusement, which
was frequented both by healthy and sick, and in
the absence of the restraints which were still felt
in the capital, every kind of indulgence was freely
practised there, so that Seneca calls it "diver-
sorium vitiorum." The bath was a very favourite
prescription with ancient physicians.

We will conclude this chapter by a short account
of the games and other amusements popular in
this period. The chief time at which these took
place was just before the bath. We have mentioned the ball-courts and galleries which surrounded the great thermæ. These were filled
with players, anxious to take exercise before their
bath. The nature of the games played in the
sphæristeria has never been quite decided, but it
appears to have been rather puerile. Three kinds
of balls were used, which were called respectively
follis, paganica, and *pila trigonalis,* the first being
the largest. The commonest game was called
datatim ludere, in which the players stood in a
circle and threw the ball to one another to catch,

* Ischia, the modern substitute for Baiæ, seems to have been
little visited by the ancients.

changing the direction unexpectedly, in order to take the receiver unawares. Plautus, however, mentions *datores* and *factores* as the two parties in a ball-game. This would suggest some game more like cricket or rounders, but we cannot follow up the clue. Another game was called *harpasta*, which seems to have been a rough scramble for the ball. The phrase *expulsim ludere* probably refers to the *datatim* game. Another favourite exercise preparatory to the bath was to fence with a blunt sword against a post. Dumb-bells were used for the same purpose of exercise before bathing.

Field-sports were popular among some classes at Rome. Coursing was the most common, the hare being followed on foot, but often snared in nets. The wild boar was also hunted with dogs. Fishing was a favourite amusement, both with bait and fly. The latter invention has been denied to the Romans by some writers, but it is proved by Martial.*

A more quiet amusement was the game of *morra*, still played in Italy. One person held up one or more fingers for a moment, and the other had to guess how many he had held up. Hence the pro-

* Ep. 5. 18, 6.

verb for an honest man, "One with whom you could play *morra* in the dark."

Games of chance were extremely popular. The chief was played with the ordinary dice (*tesseræ*) and dicebox (*fritillus*), and was generally a vehicle for gambling. When the game was πλεισ-τοβολίνδα, in the Greek phrase, sixes was the best throw; the more common mode of reckoning gave the first place to the "*Venus,*" where all the dice were different, and the worst to the "*Canis*" (four aces). Besides the dice, games were played with knuckle-bones (*tali*), which were only marked on four sides. The words "Venus" and "Canis" belong chiefly to these, which were more used than dice at banquets, in order to decide who should be the *arbiter bibendi*. Dice were forbidden by law, but, like other enactments of the same kind, the prohibition was disregarded.

Two or three games are mentioned resembling our draughts or chess. One was called "*latrunculi,*" in which the object was to take the enemy's pieces, and check-mate him (*ad incitas redigere*). There appears to be some doubt whether the game was decided like chess, or whether the player who had most pieces left at the end was the winner.* Another game of the same kind was the "*duodecim scripta*," which appears to have closely resembled backgammon. It was played with white and black pebbles (*calculi*), and combined chance and skill. Men who could not use their advantages were likened to lucky but unskilful dice-players, who made good throws, but could not play their pieces properly. The game of "noughts and crosses" was also played, "in quâ vicisse est continuasse suos."

We need not delay over children's games, which are much the same in every age and country. Hoops, tops, nuts,† and dolls were all familiar to the Roman child, and were sometimes held out as inducements to learning by the more gentle type of schoolmaster. We also hear of hide and seek (κρυπτίνδα παίζειν), forfeits, "kiss-in-the-ring," and " French and English."

* The most probable explanation of the game is that given by a writer in the "Cornhill Magazine," vol. 20. "Pieces were taken," he says, "not by being exposed to attack, but by being enclosed between two of the adversary's pieces, so that they could not be moved out of check. When no piece could be moved, the player was said, 'ad incitas redigi,' and lost the game." If this explanation is correct, the game must often have resulted in a "stale-mate," and in this case perhaps the player who had most pieces left won the game. Becker's explanation is substantially the same.

† Nuts were used instead of marbles.

CHAPTER X.

—◆—

L U X U R Y.

No feature in the life of Rome at this epoch is more persistently brought before us than the inordinate development of luxury. It was the feature which most impressed the Romans themselves, as we see by the writings of every author whose works have come down to us. Juvenal, Seneca, and the elder Pliny, the two latter especially, are vehement in their denunciations of the unheard-of extravagance which had arisen in their age. Other writers, whose principles did not lead them to deplore the change, were fully alive to it. It was recognized by all as the main characteristic of the time, as a social change, hardly less important than the political change which accompanied it.

The observations of contemporaries are to a great extent borne out by the facts as far as we know them. There is no doubt that the century which followed the battle of Actium, comprising the reigns of the Cæsarean family, did witness the highest point which luxury reached in the Roman Empire. The subject of Roman luxury in general thus belongs particularly to the period which we are considering, and deserves to be dealt with in a separate chapter. It is a very interesting subject, for the luxury of a nation is the measure of its material civilisation, as its literature is of its intellectual. The life of the wealthiest class supplies us with most of the materials which we want for comparing one civilisation with another, and we commonly even estimate the prosperity of a nation by the amount of money which is consumed in unproductive expenditure.

The opinion of Goethe on Roman civilisation is well known. In more than one place he says that the Romans always remained parvenus, who did not know how to spend their wealth, and that their luxury was nothing but tasteless extravagance and vulgar ostentation. It will be the chief object of this chapter to examine this view in the light of facts, and thus to arrive at a just estimate of both the extent and character of Roman luxury.

Before entering into detail, one or two general

remarks must be made. It has become a common-
place to contrast the extravagance and ostentation of Roman civilisation with its ignorance of
some of the simplest means of comfort. It would
be a hasty view which should condemn that
civilisation as vulgar on this account. Our civilisation is industrial; that of Rome was (to use
Herbert Spencer's distinction) militant. An industrial people both values comfort more, and is
more apt to devise means to secure it. We in
England should also remember that southern nations have always cared less than ourselves for those
minor luxuries which make up what we call comfort; and that our own ideas of what constitutes
comfort have undergone a rapid change during the
last century. The discovery of America, and the
opening of the whole world to trade, have contributed, with other causes, to raise our standard
of the necessaries of civilised life higher than
was possible to the Romans. We must then be
fully prepared to find a great inferiority in these
respects in ancient Rome, and to ascribe the defi-
ciency not to the want of proportion and "savoir
faire" which marks vulgar prosperity, but to the
causes above mentioned, which made it impossible

for civilisation to advance much further on this side.

The most imposing feature of Roman luxury is certainly the magnificence of the buildings. Here, if anywhere, Rome may challenge modern Europe to rival her splendour. The world will probably never see another Colosseum, perhaps never a second Hadrian's villa. It would, indeed, be a childish error to measure the triumphs of architecture by size alone, a criterion which would set the makers of the pyramids at Cairo and Uxmal, and of the Great Wall of China, above the men who built St. Peter's and Cologne Cathedral; but though the edifices of the Roman Empire never equalled those of Egypt in size, nor Gothic cathedrals in design, nor the works of modern engineers in practical utility, they probably exhibit, taken as a whole, a more perfect combination of these three qualities than the world has seen at any other time. The public buildings in Rome itself hold the first place. The ruins of the Colosseum and of the Baths of Caracalla, both buildings raised for luxury, perhaps impress the modern inquirer more than any descriptions of sumptuous banquets or gorgeous dress. They are on a scale quite beyond any similar buildings now existing. They imply a command of labour and material beyond the resources of the richest sovereign or corporation. (As the visitor tries to restore in his mind's eye the marble pillars, the statues, the profuse decorations in gold, silver, and costly stones, the fountains, arcades, pictures, and libraries, of the thermæ, or the magnificence of the amphitheatre in its original state, even the majesty of St. Peter's seems to sink into insignificance before these pleasure-grounds of Cæsar's subjects.) And all this beauty and magnificence was open to the poorest citizen, either absolutely gratis, or for the smallest nominal sum. It is characteristic of Rome that its noblest public buildings should be places of amusement rather than religious edifices ; these latter cannot compare with the triumphs of mediæval architecture, though many will still prefer the simple grandeur of the Pantheon, shorn as it is of its gilded roof and marble statues, to the tawdrier decoration of later churches. The wonderful roads and aqueducts which justly excite our admiration for the people who produced them, do not come under the head of luxury ; but a reference to them here cannot be omitted, before we leave the subject of Roman public buildings.

The private houses of the wealthy nobles were on a scale corresponding to the public buildings. Like them, they date chiefly from the establishment of the empire. The palace of Lucullus, which, when it was built, was the finest house in Rome, was in a few years surpassed by not less than a hundred new mansions, which vied with each other in size and splendour. Here again it is probable that modern times have failed to equal the first century of our era. The town house of the English or Continental nobleman is not now comparable to a " small city," however splendid its interior may be. There is not the need to accommodate an army of slaves under the great man's roof, nor does Western civilisation affect the spacious reception rooms and ante-rooms which the Roman nobles, like some Oriental grandees, always provided for their numerous clients and humble friends. On the other hand, the private apartments of the Roman were usually on a humble scale. The bedrooms and private sitting rooms seem to have been usually small and simply furnished. The splendour and ostentation was

chiefly reserved for the *atria* and *peristyles*, which
were adorned with marble columns, wall-paintings,
and statues, and must have presented a very imposing appearance.   There is something Oriental
about the whole arrangement of the Roman house,
with its open courts, its spacious halls, its prodigality of space, combined with very imperfect
arrangements for privacy and comfort.   If we
attempt to make for ourselves a plan of one of
these mansions from the very imperfect and con-
tradictory records which have come to us, we shall
probably end by echoing Martial's criticism of one
of them.

"Atria longa patent ; sed nec cenantibus umquam
Nec somno locus est ; quam bene *non* habitas."*

The dining-room was, however, not usually forgotten.   In great houses there was commonly
more than one *triclinium* of convenient size for
entertainment, and these were of course decorated
with great prodigality.   Besides sleeping apartments, traces have been found at Pompeii of
ante-rooms joining the bedrooms, which might
serve either as dressing rooms or private sitting
rooms.†   In exceptional cases luxury invaded

* Mart. xii. 50.
† Mentioned also by Pliny (Ep, 2. 17).

these chambers also, and the rich man provided himself with different bedrooms for different seasons, sumptuously fitted up with reference to varying temperature. But this form of luxury was, as we have said, uncommon. The bed-chamber was generally small and simple, and the " fireside " comforts neglected, as they always are where the climate permits and invites an outdoor life.

We have mentioned the wide area covered by these *domus.* The space was not always entirely occupied by the series of courts and extensive offices which formed the ordinary ground-plan of the Roman house. The rich man of the early empire was sometimes not content unless he was the possessor of a perfect *rus in urbe,** and could surround his town-house not only with trees, gardens, and shaded walks, but even with woods and vineyards, shutting out all the sounds, and even the sight of the streets. These parks in the city were, of course, few in number, and chiefly in the suburbs, or just outside the town. Many of the best houses, which were built on the Seven Hills themselves, must have had little or no gardens except within the spacious courts which the mansion itself inclosed.

* Mart. 12. 57. 21.

It is not the least of the difficulties which surround the Roman topographer to reconcile the
wide area occupied by these great houses with
the comparatively small extent of the whole
city.*

The palaces of some of the emperors of course
far surpassed the grandest private houses in size
and magnificence. To pass over the more modest
buildings of the first princes, the " Golden House "
of Nero seems to have been in design, if not in
completion, the most stupendous dwelling-place
ever built for a mortal man. Even if we regard
the ancient descriptions of the size of this palace
as greatly exaggerated,—and some of them are
without doubt intentionally so,—it remains one of
the largest royal houses ever built, and the internal
decorations seem to have been incomparably magnificent. It was surrounded by parks, woods, and
pools of great size, which seem to have been

---

* The statement of Becker (Gallus, p. 280, English ed.) as to
the great lowness of the Roman palace seems to require some
modification. Cf. Mart. 12. 57. 20, " Cui plana summos despicit
domus montes," and 4. 64. 10, " Celsæ culmina villæ," &c. If a
second and third storey were usual, the difficulty of accounting
for the space required is diminished. Friedländer, however, is
convinced that it never had a second storey in the middle, and
sometimes not even in the wings.

entirely within the walls. The colonnades of the house itself extended a Roman mile in length, and crossed some of the chief thoroughfares of the city. The cities of the East were ransacked for masterpieces of Greek art for the interior. The walls shone with gold and pearls, and the roof rested on marble columns of enormous size and beauty. If we put any faith in the accounts which have reached us, we must admit that the world then saw the crowning monument of the luxury of rulers and the servility of their subjects.

The palace of Domitian was the next in splendour to the Golden House. It was so profusely adorned with the precious metal, that a beholder might fancy the emperor possessed of the magic touch, which converts everything to gold. Plutarch and Statius give us glowing accounts of a magnificence very similar to that we have described in Nero's palace.

The country houses of the wealthy Romans were not less magnificent than the town palaces which we have just described. Every part of Italy was covered by their parks and villas. The beautiful coast of Campania, the Sabine Hills, the lakes of

the north, and every other attractive district in the
peninsula, were full of these seats.   Most rich men
were not content with one villa, but bought several
in various parts of the country, which they visited
at different seasons of the year.   Immense sums
were spent on the purchase of estates, and still
greater on laying them out.   Statius gives us an
extravagant account of the extent to which hills
were levelled and reservoirs excavated to please
the fancy of the owner.   Even the sea was
encroached upon by moles and earthworks, so
that in the rather absurd phrase of Horace, the
fish are cramped for room by the diminution of the
ocean.   This particular fancy was chiefly indulged
in the Bay of Naples, where the fashionable world
carried on many of its amusements on the water.
The ground about the house was laid out in an
elaborate and rather too artificial manner, the trees
being frequently cut into fantastic shapes, and
planted in straight rows or patterns, while the
flowers were also arranged with great care.   We
need not doubt, however, that the Romans shewed
good taste in the arrangement of their gardens as
well as in their choice of situations.   The descriptions of Pliny and Statius, who are our chief

authorities, shew that these writers had a keen
appreciation of the simple beauties of nature.
Pliny has given us a description of two of his villas,
the Tuscan and the Laurentine, the account of the
latter being admirably clear. The discovery of a
suburban villa at Pompeii has thrown much light
on his remarks and on certain obscure points in
the construction of the villas. These and other
minor sources of information are open to us, but
no one has yet succeeded in drawing a satisfactory
plan of one these immense houses, which must have
resembled a small village or a public institution
rather than a single residence. We hear of rooms
for every part of the day and each season of the
year, of long corridors and verandahs connecting
the detached portions of the house, of baths and
tennis-courts, besides all the necessary out-houses
and offices, very extensive in an establishment of
slaves. Symmetry and compactness appear not to
have been studied by the Roman architect, and the
descriptions we have mentioned, though giving us
a clear idea of each part, baffle our attempts at
arrangement. With regard to internal decoration,
it is interesting to contrast the comparative simplicity of Pliny's villa with the luxury and osten-

tation displayed in that of Manlius Vopiscus, the
subject of Statius' Eulogy.* The former was adorned
only with the cheaper kinds of marble, and common pictures and statuary; the latter blazed with
gilded beams supported by pillars of African marble,
and contained statues in silver and in bronze from
the hand of Myron. Ivory and jewels were mingled
with the precious metals in many a curiously
wrought ornament, and streams of pure water
coursed through every room, diffusing a grateful
murmur and pleasant coolness. Apparently as
much care was taken in the decoration of a
favourite villa as in that of a house at Rome. The
comparative simplicity of Pliny's was owing to his
limited fortune. We may suppose, however, that
when a rich man possessed five or six villas, as was
often the case, he confined himself to decorating
one or two only in the splendid manner above
described. Very likely works of art and ornaments were carried by the owner from one house
to another.

An interesting comparison has been made be-

* Stat. Silv. 1. 3.   Cf. also 2. 2, where he describes the Surren-
tine villa of Pollius Felix. The same magnificence of internal
decoration is described, and the baths, temples, and porticoes
close to the Bay are praised with great beauty.

tween the villas of the early Roman empire and the country houses of the nobility in this country. The conclusion come to is that the Romans far surpassed us in the profusion of costly materials used in internal decoration, while in size the Roman villa probably sometimes exceeded the largest of English castles. On the former of these points there can be no doubt. Never, perhaps, except in the palaces of the Incas, has gold been so freely used in the decoration of walls and ceilings as at Rome; never, certainly, have marbles and ivory been so lavishly employed. On the other hand, the parks and gardens of the Romans seem never to have equalled those of modern England. Partly from want of appreciation of open park-land, partly from paucity of shrubs and flowers, neither park nor garden was in keeping with the splendour within. The flowers were of simple kinds, and lacked variety, but they were grown in large quantities, for the graceful custom of wearing garlands, and even the rites of religion, made a constant and plentiful supply necessary. Roses, lilies, and violets, were the only flowers cultivated on a large scale. Greenhouses and hothouses for flowers and fruit were first introduced in our period, and of course were soon very common. Winter grapes and melons were grown under glass, and we hear of forced* roses and lilies. Fruit trees were planted sometimes among the other trees, sometimes in orchards. The Romans were well supplied with fruit. They had several kinds of apples, no less than thirty sorts of pears; plums, peaches, pomegranates, cherries, figs, quinces, nuts, chestnuts, medlars, mulberries, almonds, and strawberries. Their ornamental trees were few in number, and this doubtless led to the artificial shaping before alluded to, which was carried to absurd lengths at the close of the first century. The garden was always intersected by a path which could be used for riding, walking, or taking the air in a litter. Porticoes for lounging in the open air, and elaborate baths, were comforts not likely to be forgotten in Italy.

We naturally pass from the architecture and decoration of the Roman house to its furniture. It is necessary here to repeat the warning given before against too hasty generalisation from a few instances of great extravagance. Fancy prices are a feature of every advanced civilisation. At Rome

* "Festinatæ," Mart. 13. 127. See also on this subject, Mart. 8. 14; 4. 21. 5.

they never reached such a pitch as in modern England, where three thousand pounds have been given for a scarce old volume, but they were quite out of proportion to the ordinary scale of value. The chief crazes were for ornaments in silver plate executed by famous artists, for tables of the African wood called *citrus*, and for vases and other vessels of *murra*, which has been identified with porcelain, but is probably fluor spar. Corinthian bronzes were also bought at immense prices. As instances of the sums given for these articles, we hear that Nero paid a million sesterces for a cup of *murra*, and even Cicero the same sum for a *citrus* table. It was common to make large collections of these favourite ornaments, especially of *citrus* tables, which were admired for their beautiful grain, resembling a tiger's or panther's skin, or a peacock's tail. Seneca possessed no fewer than 500 of these tables!

Men who did not care to be in the fashion might of course furnish their houses luxuriously at far lower prices than the examples just given might seem to imply. Imitations of all kinds, such as common tables veneered with *citrus*, and silver vessels falsely fathered on some old master, were

as common as similar work in modern times ; and
even genuine ornaments which did not happen to
be in fashion were much less expensive. Still I
think Friedländer goes too far when he says that
a million sesterces was " enough to furnish luxuriously a house, perhaps a palace." He bases the
statement entirely on a passage in Martial (3. 62),
where this sum is given as the cost of the furniture
of an extravagant man, who boasted that he had
the best of everything. Martial, however, says
nothing about a large house, and tells us expressly
that the amount of furniture was small (*non
spatiosa supellex*). It seems a mistake therefore
to infer from this that ordinary furniture was "very
moderate" in price at Rome. As an instance to
the contrary, Pliny (Nat. Hist. 36. 24) says that
when the house of Scaurus was burnt down by his
slaves, he lost in the fire no less than a hundred
million sesterces. Scaurus was a millionaire and
excessively prodigal; still, so large a sum could
hardly have been spent on a house unless materials
and workmanship were dear.

Some of these costly articles of luxury were
exceedingly beautiful ; others were certainly in bad
taste. The Corinthian bronzes and the silver work

by Greek masters were of exquisite workmanship, superior without doubt in design and execution to anything now produced. The same superiority has been claimed for the work in glass and crystal, the colouring of which was an art thoroughly understood by the Romans. The remains of their glass-ware that have been dug up, faded and broken as they mostly are, testify to a very high degree of excellence. On the other hand, gilt and silver legs to the beds, and purple coverlets embroidered with pictures, seem to our taste rather barbaric. Pillows covered with silk, and mattresses stuffed with eider-down, reveal the effeminacy of the age.

These luxuries were of course confined to a few. Wealth was probably more diffused in the middle of the first century than at the close of the republic, but owing to its unproductive expenditure it failed at all times to call into being a well-to-do middle class. Plate was owned by a fairly large number of persons, and seems to have been valued as a mark of respectability, but the other extravagances we have mentioned were only to be found in the palaces and villas of the rich, who formed a very small fraction of the population, even at

R

Rome, and were rarely to be found at all in any provincial town.

Next to the dwelling and its furniture, the chief instrument of human vanity is dress. In this respect the Romans compare favourably with modern Europe. The simplicity of primitive costume was never displaced by the growth of luxury; and in spite of the costliness of some of the materials, it was almost impossible for a Roman to ruin himself, as many have done in modern times, in this most foolish form of extravagance.

The original national dress of the Romans was the toga, a woollen garment of circular shape, which was folded round the body in a peculiar manner. At first the toga was the only garment worn by either sex, but long before the end of the republic it had ceased to be worn by respectable women, and men wore the *tunica* underneath it. It remained always the distinctive dress of the Roman citizen, and its use was forbidden even to exiles and persons who had lost their civic rights. Its awkward shape, however, made it unsuitable either for work or amusement, and the custom of discarding it, except on certain occasions, was generally adopted. In the house the tunic was

generally worn alone ; out of doors it was supplemented with a *pœnula* or *lacerna*, the former of
which was often worn over the toga, for warmth.
Augustus tried to restore the use of the toga, but the
love of comfort was too strong for him, and except
at public games or ceremonies, and at court, it was
not much worn. The tunic was a white woollen
shirt, with purple stripes, these latter being by law
a badge of rank, but frequently worn with a slight
difference by others. Long sleeves and a long
skirt to the tunic were considered effeminate and
disreputable. Bright colours were popular at
Rome, and *lacernæ* of scarlet or purple were commonly thrown over the shoulder in the streets,
more for show than warmth. The toga was also
sometimes dyed, but the coveted Tyrian purple
was reserved for the emperor. It was the use of
this dye that constituted a large part of Roman
luxury in dress. There were several qualities in use,
the best being exceedingly costly. A mantle dyed
with true Tyrian purple cost, it seems, about 10,000
sesterces. The inferior kinds of purple, and other
colours, such as scarlet, blue, or green, were
cheaper, but the cost of dyeing seems to have been
always considerable. The material, however, sel-

dom cost much, for the use of wool for the ordinary garments was universal. Linen and cotton were manufactured, and pages were sometimes dressed in linen tunics, but it was not till the later empire that linen became a regular material of dress. The introduction of silk was a new luxury in our period. It was brought from India, China, and other Eastern countries, and was worth its weight in gold. Garments woven of this material were almost transparent, and were therefore justly reprobated as indecent and unbecoming. Their use by men was forbidden by law. In our period stuff of pure silk was unknown, linen and cotton being mixed with it. Gold or silver tissue, though known, was little used.

The dress of the wealthy Roman was therefore simple in form, and homely in material. Only in colour does luxury assert itself. Some extravagance was shewn in frequent changes of clothes, especially of the dinner suit, called *synthesis*. A vulgar rich man sometimes changed this several times in the course of a banquet, nominally for the sake of coolness, but really for ostentation. But this form of extravagance was not carried nearly so far as in the middle ages and modern times. Nor do we find, as we might expect, trousers introduced at Rome. Delicate or effeminate persons wrapped their legs in bandages for warmth, but *braccæ* were scouted as the most distinctive mark of barbarism, just as their absence is among ourselves. Felt hats of the simplest kind were the only coverings for the head, unless the wearer preferred to hide his face under a hood.

Hitherto we have spoken only of the men's dress. The women wore a tunic like that of the men, over which was a long robe reaching to the feet, with a flounce sewn on beneath. The same simple material was used throughout, but bright colours were usually worn in our period, perhaps almost displacing the old white stola. Purple seems to have been worn, but not of the imperial hue, and we hear of several other colours, such as green, light blue, cherry-colour, and violet. Patterns in colours were introduced about this time, and greatly admired. The process of " watering " fabrics seems to be alluded to by Pliny (Hist. Nat. 8. 48. 74.) In gold and jewellery more extravagance was displayed. These ornaments were of the usual kind, earrings, necklaces, rings, armlets, &c., and were often executed with great

S

taste. A beautiful necklace was found at Pompeii,
consisting of a gold twine supporting seventy-one
pendants, and set with rubies at the clasp.   Pearls
were much valued, and very costly.   One which
Julius Cæsar gave to Servilia cost him six millions
of sesterces. Diamonds were rare. The chief
one we know of is mentioned by Juvenal as the
property of Berenice, sister of Herod of Judæa.
This was worn on a ring ; but Juvenal says in
another place that it was fashionable to use the
best jewels in drinking cups, a custom which caused
the owner some anxiety at dinner if he could not
trust his guests.   We have already mentioned the
strange and rather barbaric use of pearls and precious stones in adorning the walls and ceiling of
rooms.   In Nero's palace there were private
chambers almost covered with pearls. We hear
also of jewels being worn on the shoes, and in the
hair, probably attached to pins.

It remains to speak of the lowest form in which
luxury shows itself—the pleasures of the table.
We have learnt to associate ideas of excessive
gluttony with the early empire, and to regard that
period as the acme of this brutish vice. A candid
investigation will reduce this censure within juster

limits. It may seem a poor form of apology to compare Roman greediness with the excesses of modern society, and cap the *cena* of Trimalchio with the menu of a Lord Mayor's banquet; it will be more to the purpose to shew that such enormities were confined to a small class during a short period, and that while the majority always fared simply, even the world of fashion was capable of repentance and self-reform.

The Romans of the republic—before the great conquests had corrupted ancient simplicity—lived with an almost ascetic frugality. The national dish was a mess of porridge (*puls*), and the generic name of *pulmentarium* served for anything that was added to it as a relish. When a cook was employed, he was the cheapest and most worthless of slaves. Drunkenness was rare, and wine, when drunk, was diluted with water. These simple habits began to be superseded after the Asiatic conquests which followed the second Punic war. A vigorous stand was made by moralists and patriots of the old school against the growth of this extravagance, but neither precept nor legislation availed to check the advancing tide. Italy, which had formerly easily supported its thrifty

population, became the importer of delicacies from
every quarter of the known world. Each new
conquest added fresh luxuries to the gourmand's
table, and gastronomy soon began to take rank
as a science. It would be tedious and unnecessary
to trace, in detail, the progress of the culinary art.
It reached its acme in the first century of the
empire, and declined after the accession of Vespasian. The period between the battle of Actium
and the death of Nero witnessed the greatest
excesses which it produced, some of which, from
their unequalled displays of gluttony, have led
historians to exaggerate the extent of the vice in
general. We should do the Romans great injustice if we were to regard the orgies of Vitellius
as characteristic of his countrymen. They were
the excesses of a miserable debauchee unexpectedly thrust into supreme power, and are never
recorded by Roman writers except with horror
and disgust. It was not the custom of Roman
officials to employ the legionaries in hunting for
rare animals and birds for the table, though the
gourmand seldom failed to profit by each new
acquisition of territory. The stories told of
Vitellius are not merely unusual but unparallelled,

unless it be in the life of his imitator, Heliogabalus.
Putting these aside, therefore, and taking the ordinary habits of the upper class as our standard, let
us consider whether we are justified in regarding
gluttony as a vice peculiarly characteristic of
Roman civilisation. The question will be best
answered by a brief survey of the meals which
formed part of the ordinary day among the
wealthy.

Soon after rising, a light breakfast, called *jentaculum*, consisting of bread, grapes, &c., was taken.
Then followed a late déjeuner, or early lunch, at
which meat, fish, eggs, &c. were placed on the
table. The dinner (*cena*) began as early as three
o'clock in the afternoon, and consisted of several
courses. Eggs, shellfish of various kinds, fish, birds
and vegetables, wild-boar and other joints, hare,
capons, and fancy dishes of many kinds, were commonly served up.* The meal was protracted for
several hours. Pliny the Elder, a man noted for
abstemious and laborious habits, rose from dinner
"before dark in summer, and soon after nightfall in
winter." This left at least three hours for the meal,

---

* See Macrob. 2. 9, for the menu of a pontifical banquet. The
feasts given by the priestly colleges seem to have been very
splendid, sometimes forming epochs in the study of gastronomy.

if it began at the usual time, and men of fashion gave much more time to it. Sometimes a banquet was protracted even till the morning light, although it had begun before the usual hour.

It is obvious that we have here the habits of a thoroughly idle as well as wealthy and luxurious aristocracy. Business was over so early in the day that the whole afternoon and evening could be given up to amusement. An invitation to dinner was supposed to include the whole day from three or thereabouts till late at night. And this inordinate space of time seems really to have been spent, if not in actual eating and drinking, yet generally in reclining at table. When we remember that a fairly substantial meal, the prandium, had shortly preceded the dinner, we must admit that the amount of food consumed seems to be excessive. And this is confirmed by Seneca and other writers. Seneca in a striking passage (Cons. ad Helv. 9), declaims against the gluttony that collects from Parthia and the Phasis delicacies which it disdains to digest—*" Edunt ut vomant, vomunt ut edant.* The coarse practice here referred to cannot be excused as a common hygienic precaution ; for though it doubtless averted to some extent the consequences of excess, it could never have been recommended or practised after a moderate repast. If, as seems certain, the Romans employed it habitually, we can only conclude that they habitually ate more than was necessary or wholesome.

To turn from the quantity to the quality of the food consumed, we are less struck by the variety and costliness of the viands than by the vulgar ostentation which shewed itself in providing them. Dishes had a fictitious value through their rarity. Thus a mullet which when of the ordinary size was cheap, commanded sometimes as much as 6,000 sesterces when it attained an unusual weight. Wild boars were served up whole. Peacocks, though not of very good flavour, were placed on the table with their tails spread. Dishes composed of the livers or brains alone of some bird or animal, were much prized, chiefly on account of their extravagant costliness. A banquet was not a success unless it was the talk of the town. The greater the waste, the more absurd the extravagance of the feast, the more certain was the giver to win the notoriety he coveted. Expense was so far from being avoided, that it was an object in itself. Hence some of the wildest stories of extravagance must be set down, not to gluttony, but to the slightly less degraded passion for ostentation. This vulgar craze was shown not less in the accessories of the banquet. Tricks and surprises, devised by the ingenuity of the cook, had the same object. Pantomimes, rope dancers, even gladiators were introduced between the courses. Flowers and ornaments of all kinds were employed with great profusion. The attendants and cupbearers were slaves chosen for their beauty, and bought at immense prices. In a word, nothing was omitted which could gain for the host a name for reckless prodigality.

It would be easy to collect instances from modern Europe of gluttony and extravagance seemingly greater than we hear of at Rome. The variety of dishes at a modern banquet is much greater, the cost may be more, than in the early empire. But it is a mistake to argue from such instances that the luxury of the table is really greater now than then. Such a theory will not bear examination. Modern banquets, however much they may pass the limits of justifiable indulgence, do not occupy half the entire day, and the triumphs of the kitchen are not an approved subject of conversation in ordinary society. If we have gone further in ordinary discoveries, the Roman gourmand was inferior only through circumstances, not from taste or moderation. So far as we can see, after making all deductions for exaggeration and peculiar cases, the wealthiest class at Rome must bear the reproach of excessive addiction to the pleasures of the table, and of coarse vulgarity in the pursuit of them.

The extenuating circumstances must be sought elsewhere. In the first place, the number of persons able to give first-rate banquets was necessarily very small ; and outside this narrow circle it appears that the old frugal habits had not entirely disappeared. In the provincial towns, and among the middle and lower classes in the capital, men were content with the modest fare which is most suited to the climate of Italy. Meat was eaten sparingly, and the staple diet consisted of grain, fruit, and eggs. The second vindication of the Roman character on this head is to be found in the fact that it was still capable of self-reform. The example and precepts of a frugal emperor only brought to light a change in public opinion which was ready to shew itself. Many causes had combined to produce a feeling of satiety and disgust at the manner of life which society had been leading. Men were anxious to rise above the coarse animalism of the last fifty years, and a sumptuary reform seemed the first and most obvious step. Another cause was at work in the diminution of wealth, which was now perceptible. The policy of the empire had closed some of the avenues of fortune, and the privileged class, which had so long lived and rioted on the capital of the world, began to find that their mine was not inexhaustible. Accordingly a decided, though gradual, movement in the direction of simplicity began after the accession of Vespasian. Extravagance ceased to be fashionable. Many curtailed the expenses of their table from principle, after the manner of the Stoic philosophy; others sought to please their guests rather by the good taste and appropriateness of the repast than by its profusion or expense. Counter reactions indeed took place before the end of the century, but never produced so much excess as had been witnessed in its earlier part.

We have now considered Roman luxury in its most important aspects, as they appeared in the first century of our era. The most important omission is that of slavery, which was of course the greatest instrument of luxury, and gave a character to all the rest. The subject has, however, been treated of in a former chapter, and it must be sufficient here to refer to what was there said of the use of slaves for purposes of luxury. We should now be able to form some generalisations from the facts stated in this chapter, and to estimate the character and extent of Roman luxury at this period. From the material point of view we have said that in magnificent buildings, both public and private, later centuries have failed to outstrip the earlier empire. In internal decoration we mentioned the extraordinary profusion of rare marbles and precious metals, and the passion for certain favourite articles of furniture or ornament. We drew attention to the semi-Oriental character of the house arrangement, and the sacrifice of comfort to ostentation which seems to characterise it. Passing to dress, we admired the comparative simplicity of attire which we find at Rome, and noticed especially the universal use of the commonest materials. Lastly, we deplored the coarse luxury of the table, and on comparing the first century with the

nineteenth, decided that though the apparatus of
gluttony was less, the tendency to excess and
over-indulgence was greater than it has ever been
since. From the social point of view, we have
said that luxury, in most of its forms, was confined to a small class in the capital. This is true,
but, notwithstanding, there is a decidedly democratic side to Roman luxury. Its most splendid
monuments, the baths and amphitheatre, were
built for the delectation of the masses. Its grandest
public works, its roads and aqueducts, were works
of universal utility. If, in one sense, it was restricted to a smaller number than in modern
societies, in another it was more accessible to
every one than has often been the case since.
We must not lose sight of this good side of the
subject, for it is both significant in itself, and a useful corrective of the indiscriminate censure which
has sometimes been heaped upon pagan civilisation. Self-indulgence and extravagance shewed a
more unblushing front before the rise of Christianity;
but it is doubtful whether religion is any real
check to the luxury of our great capitals. The
main features are the same as those of Roman
civilisation, the chief difference being in the indus-

trial type stamped upon our society as opposed to the semi-Oriental character of the Roman. Our luxury is the product of national labour, the spending of wealth created from year to year by the industry of the people ; that of Rome was the luxury of a dominant caste, which found itself almost suddenly in command of the resources of three continents, resources which it used unscrupulously for its own benefit, without attempting to restore the waste. It is true that a luxurious class is alway unproductive, but the complete severance of that class at Rome from the producers had a strong influence on its character, and caused those vulgarisms of extravagance which give colour to Goethe's criticism quoted above. On the whole, however, we think that the German poet's censure goes too far, and that we are not justified in passing a sweeping condemnation on the luxury of the first century of our era, on the ground either of excess or of bad taste.

CONCLUSION.

WE have now completed our sketch of Roman society in the first century. The magnitude of the subject has compelled us to treat each part of it in a cursory manner, but it is hoped that no important or characteristic feature has been omitted. We ought now to be able to stand back, as it were, from the picture, and form some kind of general impression from it. Shall we agree with Gibbon, who considered that under good emperors, such as the series beginning with Nerva at the close of our period, " the human race " was more happy and prosperous than at any other epoch in the world's history ? The idea will hardly meet with a defender at the present day. For who are " the human race" whose condition was so enviable ? The small coterie of millionaires, who wallowed in self-indulgence, and drained the life blood of the empire ? Or the mass of poor Italians, of heavily taxed provincials, of miserable slaves, who do not indeed fill a large space on the page of history,

but who still had the right to be reckoned among
human beings ? Was their lot so happy or so
prosperous ? And can even the intellectual voluptuary, such as Gibbon doubtless had in his mind,
excite our envy, surrounded as he was by crowds
of slaves and dependants, and by every means of
gratifying alike the highest and lowest pleasures ?
Surely not. We may grant, probably we should
grant, that the Roman understood the art of
living better than we understand it ; that he
knew better than we how to make the most of all
the pleasures under the sun, from the noblest art
to the vilest indulgences : we still feel that our
civilisation is the higher of the two, and that we
would not, if we could, exchange our restless
moral consciousness, our troubled political activity,
our busy competitive industry, for the unabashed
hedonism, the selfish indifference, the wasteful
indolence of the Roman of the early empire.
With all its brilliancy, that civilisation lacked the
vital spark ; it was soulless, faithless, and essen-
tially unprogressive. Rome had outlived her
ideals ; her patriotism and her religion had alike
become obsolete, and the renovating principle was
not to be found within her own pale. It is only

indistinctly that we can trace, in the first century, the growing influence of that contact between the religious consciousness of the East and the intellectual activity of the West, which was destined to determine the character of mediæval and modern civilisation.

THE END.

www.ingramcontent.com/pod-product-compliance
Lightning Source LLC
Chambersburg PA
CBHW020509270326
41926CB00008B/798